ABDULAZIZ

Making Yemen a Good World Citizen

Raidan ALSAQQAF

Copyright © Raidan ALSAQQAF, 2022
All Rights Reserved.
ISBN: 978-1-7388201-0-8

I dedicate this book to all of Abdulaziz's grandchildren, be proud and inspired.

- Raidan

Author's Note

This book is based on a true story, the story of my father. It has been twenty-three years in the making, it recounts life events to the best of my recollection and what I have found in my research, relying on my family history, first-hand accounts, and stories published in *Yemen Times* in print and online. This book is therefore part memoir and part literary fiction based on the memoir. I assume no responsibility toward any persons mentioned in this book, and views included are mine and do not reflect the views of any government, political group, or the United Nations. I do not guarantee the historic accuracy of mentioned events, interactions, or positions.

I would like to thank my siblings, Haifa, Walid, and Nadia, for their valuable inputs and support in putting this together, and to Ramzy Al-Saqqaf for his diligent support in digitizing and sharing archived *Yemen Times* copies. Special thanks to Ursula Acton for her editorial work, to AbdulRahman Jaber for his design support, and to my wife Rasha for standing by me throughout the journey of writing this book. I would also like to thank my late father for his example and the legacy he left us, we will eventually make Yemen a good world citizen.

If you have any notes about this book or stories about Dr Abdulaziz that you'd like to share for inclusion in a future print, please write to: r_saqqaf@yahoo.com

Raidan AlSaqqaf
25 Dec 2022
Ottawa

Cover Image released into the public domain by its author, Carlos Latuff, 2011.

Table of Contents

Part One: The Journey 7
   Chapter 1: A Day Like No Other 8
   Chapter 2: Origins 35
   Chapter 3: Taiz City 51
   Chapter 4: Finding Destiny in Sana'a 64
   Chapter 5: America Calling 74
   Chapter 6: And Back to Yemen 82
   Chapter 7: My "Human Rights" Hobby 86

Part Two: Yemen Times 96
   Chapter 8: Introducing Yemen Times 97
   Chapter 9: Tribulations of a Young Democracy 102
   Chapter 10: Turbulence begets ... Optimism? 109
   Chapter 11: Vote for Abdulaziz 115
   Chapter 12: Undemocratic Democracy 122
   Chapter 12: War 127
   Chapter 13: Hello, Mr President 138
   Chapter 14: Reconciling with Saleh 148
   Chapter 15: Elections, Round 2 155
   Chapter 16: Making Progress 160
   Chapter 17: Human Rights at the Consultative Council 169
   Chapter 18: Thieves Don't Build Nations 174
   Chapter 19: The Trial 182
   Chapter 20: The Final Lunch 196

Part One: The Journey

Chapter 1: A Day Like No Other

Few jobs scream BORING more than being a professor of economics. It was a combination of misunderstandings and luck that pulled me into this path. Actually, it was the government of the United States that made this decision for me. At the time, I had just finished my undergraduate degree in Sana'a University in English literature, and I took on a job as the first English-language television news broadcaster in the country's history. My job was simple: to make a succinct summary of the day's news, and present it in a thirty-minute segment at 11pm. It was the mid 1970s and it was the norm to read from behind the studio desk while holding a bunch of papers and sporting the obligatory mustache. You'd find me dressed in one of two standard-issue cheap suits: a shade of brown or a shade of gray. Lovely.

At the time, Yemen was divided into two countries, North and South Yemen. The South was a Marxist State allied with the Soviet Union, so naturally the West injected a concentrated dose of capitalism into the North to ward off any Marxist charms that might trickle through the border. We actually had a Citibank branch and a KFC open up in 1975, and, I must confess, the fried chicken diplomacy was a million times more effective than anything the USSR and its proxies could ever offer.

One afternoon, while I was prepping the daily news in the newsroom, our head producer, dressed in his enviable navy-blue suit, rushed to the newsroom frantically screaming my name.

"Abdulaziz... Abdulaziz. Come quick, go go. Hurry hurry. Yalla yalla..."

"Yes Sir, where are we going?" I asked.

"They called from the Presidential office. You must go to interpret for the President. Hurry, Uncle Mahmoud is waiting in the staff bus. He'll drive us there," he added.

Unbeknownst to me, both the President's official interpreter and his backup had fallen ill and lost their voices, and someone suggested that I go interpret for a meeting between our President and the US ambassador. The President always made it a point to have an interpreter on his team and not to rely purely on the other side. As luck would have it, that day the interpreter would be me. I hadn't realized that my reading the English news at 11pm would bestow such an honor upon me. My workmates at the Television Station always joked that when I come up on TV, that means it's time to turn it off and go to bed. And they were right in a sense, as the English news was the last segment to air before the broadcast was disconnected. Luckily the TV broadcasting compound wasn't too far from the Presidential palace, so we hopped into the staff bus and found our way toward the Presidential palace.

At the time, President Al-Hamdi had been in power less than a year. Coming from a military background, he had a firm hand in enforcing the rule of law and his vision for what he wanted the country to be. He was known to be both a visionary and charismatic leader, but also a serious no-nonsense military commander who didn't like to argue. His word was law and he made sure the military work ethic and strictness were adopted across all civilian government entities. He was known to make surprise visits to government entities to ensure attendance and good discipline. He once reportedly visited the Ministry of Trade on concerns of price inflation, and arrived in the morning before the Minister got there.

He went directly to the Minister's office and started going through whatever documents and reports were sitting at the Minister's desk. The Minister arrived shortly thereafter and rushed in, knowing he was in the hot seat.

As the Minister walked into his office, the President made him sit on the floor in the middle of the office, with the Vice Minister and other senior officials in attendance. Then the President asked him sarcastically:

"*Too early.... Where were you?*"

"*Mr President, welcome to the Ministry. I passed by the market to check on the prices of commodities to make sure...*" the Minister replied.

"*Ha...*" the President interrupted, adding, "*I see here requests and paperwork that date back up to two weeks. Why is this paperwork not being processed yet? Why are you holding back peoples' business?*"

"*Mr President, I was verifying and validating this information to make sure it is all accurate,*" the Minister responded.

"*Tell me then, what am I looking at?*" the President queried, pointing at the pile of paperwork on the desk.

"*There are many requests, Mr President, new contracts for food supplies and import permits...*"

"*Shush...*"[silence] "*And who goes inspecting the prices at 8am in the morning? Don't you know how the markets work? Half the vendors haven't even arrived at the markets yet.*"

Just then, an officer walked in and asked for permission to speak. "*Sir, AlFandim Khamis wishes to inform you that the Minister did not pass by the markets today, Sir.*"

"*Ahaa. And you lie to me too. Alright, give him a paper and a pen... Write down 'President Ibrahim Mohammed Al-Hamdi, has decreed that, Minister of Trade is removed from his office effective immediately, and replaced with his deputy'.*"

The President got up from behind the Minister's desk and walked out. The Minister was about to get up and follow the President, but the officer who walked said to him, "*Who allowed you to stand up? The President said sit there. You sit. AlFandim Khamis is not done with you yet.*"

AlFandim Khamis was the head of the national intelligence apparatus. AlFandim is a title inherited from the Ottoman rule, derived from the Turkish word Effendi or Afandem, which indicates rank seniority. Khamis was in effect the President's right hand for all security matters including policing civil servants and the citizenry. He was also known to be short-tempered and carried a baton looking for improperly parked cars and smashed their windows. It was a reputation that lingered after his tenure for years. Mothers warned their kids, "*I'll bring Khamis's Baton*" to threaten them into behaving.

I knew of these details and much more because I worked in media and got all the gossip in the TV's newsroom. In fact, I reported recently that the President visited the Ministry of Trade, and that he appointed a new Minister, with that story in the back of my mind. Obviously, we regularly used lots of filler material to give context, saying that the President is keen to ensure that the prices remain stable and that supply is ample to meet the needs of the people, etc. I knew these stories and those about the President's personality, another reason for me to be nervous to be called to the Presidential palace.

We arrived at the Presidential palace. I straightened my suit and used a tissue to clean my shoes, checking on my pencil, spare pen, and notepad to do a good job. There might be an opportunity for me here: I could possibly work for the President. I can't wait to go home and tell my wife, Aziza, about all of this.

This was my first time in the Presidential office, and I knew there would be some security arrangements and I would probably be searched rigorously. I prepared my identification card. It was a hand-written card with a black and white personal photo with a huge stamp over it. It was a terrible photo, with a medium-size afro-like hairdo and a lazy mustache. But hey, it was what it was. We left the bus and rushed to the gate where a soldier was waiting to escort us inside. I heard the head producer saying, "*I'm with him. I'm with him.*" Apparently the instructions were only to rush Abdulaziz the interpreter in, and nothing about anyone else, so he had to wait outside by the door.

I followed the soldier, almost running, toward the Presidential palace. It looked like a large house. I expected it to be bigger than that, honestly. We usually drove by its high fences not knowing what was inside, imagining a huge palace with all sorts of courts and buildings within it. Suddenly the soldier detoured away from pathway to the palace and into the garden, where I saw a tent with a few people sitting around a table with some tea glasses and water bottles. That was the President over there, along with the Prime Minister as well.

"*Abdulaziz. Come,*" yelled the President. "*Come sit here.*"

I tried to keep my composure and remain professional by not saying a word, but my mind was screaming: *He Knows My Name!* The

President was very charismatic, spoke eloquently, and was presidential in many ways. He portrayed a degree of humility and asked me to sit next to him, along with the Prime Minister and a Caucasian gentleman I assumed was the US Ambassador.

The President got straight to business, dictating to me the messages he would like to convey to the Ambassador after casual welcoming remarks.

"We want to deepen the friendships that are between our peoples. The American people are great people, and they achieved many great advances in science and industry. We too want to achieve such advances, we are working on our national development plan to expand agricultural productions and make further investments in infrastructure for modern industry."

The Ambassador replied, *"Of course, Mr President. Congress has approved doubling the appropriations to the Yemen development program and investing in important projects in water, education, agriculture, health, and other areas."*

"We still haven't seen much coming from your side..." the President started. Then quickly, *"Abdulaziz don't interpret that."*

"We want the United States government to help us in building an industry and manufacturing base," he continued. *"We want American businesses to invest here. We have a plan to become more industrial. We only have twenty-two factories in this country. I want to increase that number to two hundred by next year, and to one thousand the year after..."*

"Mr President," the US Ambassador interjected, *"The development and wellbeing of the Yemeni people is a priority for the United States administration, we are launching a number of*

programs to promote Yemen as a destination for American businesses and investments."

Then the Ambassador paused for a second, took a glance at me, and reluctantly continued: *"But Mr President, there are a number of important reforms that need to be made to ensure that the laws and regulations protect the interests of these potential investors, and reiterate your commitment to a free market economy."*

Although I was interpreting only, I sort-of knew what the Ambassador was hinting at. The President has recently introduced some agrarian land reforms that forcibly took away large swaths of lands from feudal landlords and distributed them among small holders through agricultural cooperatives, similar to what President Jamal Abdel Nasser introduced in Egypt not too long ago.

President Al-Hamdi interjected, *"Modernizing Yemen requires that we work in different directions at the same time, we need to move on trade, construction, and other developments to achieve our goals. Yemen has been falling behind and we need to move quickly."*

The Ambassador nodded in agreement.

"We want to show Yemenis, in North and in South, that development and prosperity are within reach, and that with the help of our friends, we can achieve them," the President said. It was obvious he was hinting at understanding the geopolitical dynamics and Yemen's own version of the cold war between the capitalist North and the Marxist South. If a unified Yemen emerged, it would want to adopt a capitalist system as it proved better than a socialist/Marxist one.

"The French," the President added, *"only speak and don't do much, but I know that the United States, as a bigger and more*

respected country, would be able to move quickly in our cooperation, I'll have the Minister of Foreign Affairs connect with you to perhaps organize a visit to America."

"*We welcome that*," the Ambassador said. "*I'll send a cable to Washington immediately to put that in motion.*"

It was clear to President Al-Hamdi that he must take action to strengthen relationships with the United States; perhaps building this relationship would help include Yemen as a key partner in the eyes of the United States in the region. Just a few months ago, President Nixon had visited four countries in the area, but not Yemen despite it being the only cold war battle ground in the region.

It was also quite insightful to me to learn first-hand how President Al-Hamdi thought, playing global and regional politics for the advancement of Yemenis. I had liked him previously for his sincere and candid approach to governing the country, but now I liked him a lot more.

The meeting with the US Ambassador didn't last long. Perhaps they had lost some time while waiting for an interpreter, but at least I enabled sending a few messages across. It felt like the meeting ended abruptly. I had hoped to shake hands again with the President, perhaps make a good impression or get my picture taken with him. Maybe even a new job or a promotion? You never know when an opportunity like this might happen again.

The President walked toward the palace and the Ambassador was escorted out of the building. I stood in my place, sort of frozen. A gentleman in a suit approached me and asked me to follow him into his office next to the gate. There I received a small cash bonus and was sent on my way.

In a sense, I was happy to be recognized, to be called for in person, and to have the opportunity to spend some time with the President. Perhaps it was foolish to let my imagination run wild and think that this would be a straight ticket to a promotion, but at least I got a cash bonus and a fantastic story to tell.

Perhaps my best takeaway was that I could tell my workmates that "Turn-off-the-TV" Abdulaziz had met the President. I was sort of an outcast in the TV station's newsroom, always snooping around to take other people's work and not doing any original journalism on my own. The news editor made two copies of each approved news item, one for the main news in Arabic, along with recorded footage, and a second for the English version of the news courtesy of Abdulaziz, which is the last thing to be broadcasted before shutting down the airwaves. *Abdulaziz, if we could make your segment even less important, we would.*

The English news was a pet project for the head of the TV station, his interpretation of modernizing and showing international relevance. I got the job because I was the highest-scoring graduate in English literature from Sana'a University last year. Working hard in school has its rewards, and I remain a bookworm deep inside.

Now I had met the President, which I hoped would mean something to elevate the importance of my work and the prominence of the English-language news broadcast. I was happy to have the head producer testify in favor of my case, I thought, as I walked out of the gate toward the waiting staff bus with the head producer in it waiting impatiently.

Suddenly, I heard someone approaching me. "*Abdulaziz... The Ambassador wants to talk to you.*"

I didn't see that coming, I thought to myself. What Ambassador? Then snapped out of my thoughts about the newsroom. Right, the

US Ambassador, of course. *I wonder what he wants. Maybe the embassy is seeking an interpreter?*

"*I would like to thank you for your interpretation, Mr Abdulaziz,*" the Ambassador said in a thick American accent. I was a bit taken back, especially the way he pronounced my name, with a thick but familiar American accent. It struck me because I had not realized that he had this accent while I was interpreting inside. Maybe I was too nervous and too focused on *what* was being said to realize *how* it was being said. But then again the President did most of the talking anyway.

"*Here, I want you to call Robert. Take care now,*" the Ambassador said, while handing me his business card with a hand-written telephone number on it.

I waved goodbye thinking to myself, *What just happened! Robert who? Call him why? What is going on?* as the Ambassador's car drove away.

Worse, the head producer had seen me take the business card, as did the guards from the Presidential palace. *God. What just happened? Now they all will think that the Americans have some sort of a relationship with me, they might even think I am an American agent. Maybe I'm doomed. Maybe this bizarre day also includes a rendezvous with AlFandem Khamis, I don't know!* I clutched the card in my palm trying to hide it, almost passing out inside while remaining on my two feet, snapping out of it when the head producer pulled my arm toward the bus.

"*Hey... Hot Shot now? You met the President? Did you ask him for an appointment? Did you tell him you have ideas to improve the TV service? Maybe he will put you as Minister of Information.*" The head producer barraged me with teaser questions. *"Don't forget who your friends are when you get to high places,"* he added

I took my seat on the staff bus and looked at the head producer dead in the eye, and said,

"Water.... Do you have any water? I'm really thirsty and my voice is lost."

"They didn't even give you a drink? All this huge palace and they wouldn't even let me in or give you some water?"

"I didn't get inside the building. The meeting was in the yard ... in the garden."

"Maybe they were painting the walls," the head producer jokingly said.

The few minutes' drive back to the office allowed me to collect my thoughts. I looked at the crumbled business card clutched in my palm. *What do I do with this now? I better hide it. If anybody asks me, I would say the Ambassador just said thank you.*

I returned to the office, where it seemed most people had not known what I was up to. The head producer went about his business. He had to make up for the hour or so he spent outside and get the schedule back on track. But I must say it was odd preparing for that evening's English-language news, especially as it mentioned the President's meeting with the US Ambassador. I wondered if the President would be watching me on TV now - unlikely though as he didn't understand English. But I was positive the US Ambassador was following the news. Little did I know that the whole embassy was watching and even relying on my work to get an insight into what was reported and other happenings of interest.

I was usually the last to leave the building at night after my segment had aired, and Uncle Mahmoud – the bus driver – would drive me home. There were usually six of us on that ride – me, whoever had the unfortunate luck to produce my segment that night, and the night cleaning crew. This evening, just before we left, Uncle Mahmoud called and whispered to me, "*The eyes are on you, don't tell anyone where you went today and what happened.*"

"*Yes, Uncle Mahmoud, I won't. Thank you*," I replied.

This was a day that refused to end. I'd come to learn in the newsroom that the phrase "the eyes are on you" was often traceable to AlFandem Khamis, but I hadn't thought that Uncle Mahmoud was also part of AlFandem Khamis's network.

I made it home just after midnight, my usual time. Usually, Aziza left me a plate of dinner to eat before I tip-toed to bed so as to not wake the kids, but after a day like that, food was the last thing on my mind. I washed my face, changed, and quietly made it to bed.

"*Aziza.... Are you awake? I met the President today.*"

"*SLEEP!*" She said.

Hello, Robert

The next morning, I woke up with the phone ringing. It was the jarring ringtone of those old rotary phones, but somehow, I thought, this call had something to do with yesterday's eventful day.

Aziza picked up the phone. *"Hello, yes, ... Okay... Okay... I will tell him."* Then she hung up the phone.

"Aziza, who was that?"

"They called from the village. They wanted to tell you that your father is coming to Sana'a."

It doesn't get any easier now, does it? I have a complicated relationship with my father to put it charitably. Still, I preferred a heads-up about my father's imminent visit to a call from AlFandem Khamis – since the eyes are on me, or whatever.

I told Aziza about the proceedings of the previous day, about how I was rushed out of the office, about the Presidential palace and meeting the President, about the things he said and what he was trying to do. About the reactions of the US Ambassador, and about the card situation, and calling Robert. I told her I was worried it might put me in a bad light, and how eyes were on me now at work, and Uncle Mahmoud's advice not to speak of what happened.

She was both proud and excited. She was always there for me, encouraging me and pushing me on. She had this unique quality in her; she never complained about anything and always resolved to address whatever challenges came her way. Whatever the problem was, Aziza would find a way to fix it. I asked for her advice on whether I should call Robert as the Ambassador asked.

"Do you think the Americans want harm or good for you?" she asked.

"I don't know, but I don't think they would want to harm me. What did I ever do to them, plus I had good relations with the American volunteers teaching at the University."

"So, call them, you never know. If it won't do you good then at least it won't harm you."

So I got my pencil and notepad, moved the phone to my lap, took a deep breath, and started calling, rotating the dial halfway. Then hanging up.

"Call! What is wrong? You don't want to call?" she asked.

"No, no, I just got mixed up with the numbers." Which was a lie. I was chickening out. I wanted to make a good phone impression and rehearse the conversation. Obviously, Aziza saw right through me, and then moved away saying, *"I'll go make you some tea."*

"Hello, my name is Abdulaziz Al-Saqqaf. I would like to speak with Mr Robert please."

"Hey Abdulaziz, how are ya? I was expecting your call. How is everything?"

"I am doing very okay, Sir." I was mumbling and realized I failed in making the good impression that I was hoping for.

"That's good. Listen, we have a new program. Come by the embassy and pick up the application forms. I want you to fill them up and send me copies of your certificates as well as your resume. Do you have a resume?" he asked. *"We'll make one for you, or*

listen, bring your passport and certificates and come to the embassy, we'll work through them together. When can you come?"

I paused, unsure what was going on. *Why does Robert want this information, why does he want me to go to the embassy? Are they head-hunting me?* I had no idea what program he was referring to or where this was going.

"*How about tomorrow? Nine o'clock?*" Robert asked.

"*Sir, why do you want me to come to the embassy?*" I had plucked up some courage.

"*For the scholarship. Why, nobody told you? We're sending you to the United States to study there. I'll explain when you get here. So 9 o'clock?*"

"*Yes, sir, I will come tomorrow at 9 o'clock in the morning.*" Being a smart-ass to confirm that it is 9 in the morning, not 9pm, because night meetings are stuff that spies will do. But this was honest business.

"*Great, see ya tomorrow,*" Robert said and hung up.

"*Bye....*" I said, to nobody on the other end of the line.

I put the phone away and spotted my telephone book. *It looks like I may be calling that number again in the future, so let me jot down the details in case I lose this crumbled card.* At that moment Aziza walked in, and asked me what they said as she handed me a small glass of red tea.

"They said they want to give me a scholarship to study in America. I have to go tomorrow to do some paperwork."

"What about your job? You can't afford to leave that job; we will lose our livelihood without your salary," Aziza said.

She was right. I was just starting my professional career, had a family to provide for. I had two young children, and must think about our future needs and family security. Things were moving on so quickly. It's been less than twenty-four hours since this whole situation unfolded. I felt like I was on an involuntary roller coaster, and I dragging everyone else with me. Yesterday my biggest concern was saving for a car and fixing the plumbing in our fixer-upper house. O how simple life was yesterday.

"Aziza..." I said, *"nothing happened yet. I'll just see what this is, and then see if it is good or not, don't worry."*

Once again, she saw right through me.

"You will go to America," she said,

"I have to go to work," I replied grudgingly. She was probably right. Opportunities like this were to be grabbed by hands and teeth, as the local idiom said.

"NO, wait," she said. *"Your father is coming, did you forget? You need to do some shopping and help me prepare. He will probably arrive before you do. Can you come early tonight?"*

"You keep asking me to come home early while you know that I can't," I replied with some frustration, knowing that my father's presence was only going to add to my strains. It was never a social visit with him, he always wanted something.

"*Here, take this cash and you figure it out.*"

"*We also need to take Haifa and Walid to the clinic for vaccines. They said the father must be there and we must take the family card,*" she added.

"*Some other time...*" I said.

I usually made it to the office around noon. My routine started by passing by the newsroom to see what the instructions for the day were. There was a huge school-style blackboard with daily items written on it with chalk. It mainly represented the headlines that would be broadcasted in the main news at 9pm. That timeslot was a two-hour segment. Sometimes it was a slow day so they had to use a lot of filler footage from field visits and archive recordings of officials meeting while on mute, or adding segments from Arab and International News wire services. That would go something like this: Palestine, somewhere else in the Arab World, some other country – and, of course, sports.

On other days, there would be so much going on that some items would be skipped. It was two hours of news with some commercials in between. I took a peek at the news schedule, ignored the spelling mistakes, then I prepared a short list of what I thought were the headlines that should make it to the English-language news broadcast. I then would go to see the head producer, around 2pm or so, the proposed outline run by him for his approval, then start working on my segment. Most of my time, I was translating the Arabic script to English, editing for brevity and clarity, and rehearsing.

"*Abdulaziz, I decided to hire someone to help you out,*" the head producer said at the beginning of our 2pm meeting. "*You have a lot of work, and we should have more people who work with you in the English news.*"

"*Thank you, Sir. And if we can have an earlier time slot in the studio as well, we could produce the news earlier as well,*" I said.

"*We'll see,*" he replied.

I sat at my desk and started to do the usual work, when I noticed that the room was quieter than usual. I didn't ask any questions or mention anything, thinking people were preoccupied or didn't want to mention the oddity of being called to the Presidential palace yesterday. Maybe they didn't want to speak in case gossip prompted someone to ask a question or say something about yesterday. This was a newsroom, after all, and the eyes were on me. Maybe that was why.

Maybe. Just maybe – since the room was quiet and everybody was minding their own business – maybe I could take some time to work on my resume? I knew what a resume was, but what would I say on mine? I took a ruler and a piece of paper, made a straight line one inch from the left side, and started writing with my best handwriting: Name. Address. Education. Experience. It looked too small with too little information. So I gave it another try, again and again.

My colleagues didn't notice; maybe they thought I was making a clean copy of an edited script, taking yet another a fresh piece of white block-note paper, making the indent line, writing and writing, and then repeating.

"*Abdulaziz,*" one of my colleagues said, "*you want a sandwich from the cafeteria?*"

"*No thanks, I'm good,*" I replied, thinking I had better get on with my work. Whatever I had so far was good enough. Tomorrow I would work with Robert and see what happened.

As I arrived home, I passed by my father asleep in the hallway, with his bag, a small basket of sorghum bushels which he bought from the village farms, as well as what looked like a bunch of opened candy wrappers. Haifa and Walid must have had a party, being spoiled by sugary treats.

Let's see what tomorrow brings, I thought. I usually slept in until 9 or 10am given my working hours, however this time I set my alarm to 6am. I might not have had a full good night's sleep, but at least I would have enough time to make it to the embassy early for my appointment. I kept running the scenario in my head over and over again until I fell asleep.

The next day I sat for breakfast with my father, with Haifa in my lap. She was used to having to stay quiet in the morning so as not to disturb my sleep, so this was a refreshing change to see her father and grandfather around, and everyone showering her with attention. She kept bringing the candy to me saying *"Baba, look. Baba, take..."* helping herself to her Grandpa's bag in search of candy and treats. She was excited as well as being on a sugar high. Walid, on the other hand, was busy roaming around in his walker.

My father and I sat on the floor around a plate of fava beans and milk tea. *"How is the village and everyone there?"* I asked him.

He leaned back, fixed his white Mashadah [shawl], around his shoulder, and said *"Everything is great, we had good rains, the crops are blossoming, and everything is going well. I brought you some sorghum bushels too, I know you like them barbecued."*

He added, *"Why don't you come to the village. This is a good time to go visit, also to check on your house there and see the people."*

Aziza had been asking for a while to go and visit, and with my work and all the commitments I just couldn't. I had to focus on my career, and in my line of work, and especially since the English news was essentially a one-man show, it was hard to take a sick day off, never mind a holiday.

"*I want you to come in the month of Sha'aban* [eighth month of the Islamic calendar], *I want you to come help me with my wedding*," he said.

I had known there would be a catch. It was never just a social call or to see his grandkids. I also felt Aziza listening in on our conversation from the kitchen, waiting for a chance to come pick up the emptied fava bean plate. I didn't know how up-to-speed she was with the village's gossip, but this news was more of a headline than gossip.

I wanted to yell at him, "*How much?*" knowing it was all about money. But I thought there would be no point in arguing with him, especially as I had to go for the appointment at the embassy.

"*I have to go to work now, let me get back to you on that. Tomorrow is the weekend, let's discuss tomorrow.*"

When it rains, it pours. So much was going on in so little time. I made it to the embassy with forty minutes to spare, just to be on the safe side. When I arrived I just loitered around, not sure if I should press ahead and walk in, or if I was just too early. As I was thinking, I saw a few people pass me and walk toward the embassy. It looked like a family – two adult males, a woman, and a young man. They got out of a taxi just a few yards away. I thought it looked like the embassy was open and people were walking into the building, so I might as well just go, too.

We stood in line at the gate, everybody preparing an ID to get into the embassy. I saw one of the men pick up the family's passports to be given to the officer allowing them entry. He was holding two types of passports, and I was curious. This looked like a mixed Yemeni-American family. How strange, none of them looked American at all. I handed over my identity card, and mentioned I had an appointment with Robert.

"*Robert who?*" the officer asked.

"*Mr Robert, the person responsible for the scholarships. Here,*" and I handed him the Ambassador's business card.

"*Please wait here*" and he guided me into the waiting room, where I joined the family.

So I sat waiting, my files in my hand, making sure my shoes were clean, and that I looked presentable. I was browsing the posters in the waiting room - there is Manhattan, and the Grand Canyon, there is also San Francisco with its iconic bridge as well. My knowledge about the United States was somewhat limited to whatever information came my way during my degree, as well as a few bits and pieces here and there of popular culture. My thoughts were interrupted by the young man asking me, "*You're going to America too?*"

"*Insha'Allah* [God willing]," I replied. I actually had no idea. Was I really going to America? I probably was, it just hadn't really sunk into my head yet.

"*Then we go to America together,*" the teenager said.

One of the adults got wind of the conversation and asked, "*Where in America are you going? Do you have family or anyone you know there?*"

"*I'm not sure,*" I replied.

"*Come to New York,*" he said, adding, "*There are many jobs there. The newlyweds are going there.*"

I was in awe. So that woman was apparently an American citizen, and came to Yemen to get married, and her family picked this young man as a husband for her? And his primary preoccupation was jobs in New York as far as I could tell.

"*Here, let me give you my number. When you come to America, call me, I'll help you find work in New York,*" the older gentleman said, tearing up a piece of paper with his number and name.

"*Oh, give it back, I'll also write the address,*" he added.

So there I was, less than ten minutes in the US Embassy, and I already had almost a job offer in New York, In Brooklyn to be specific.

"*Abdulaziz Al-Saqqaf,*" the loudspeaker said. "*Come to the window.*"

I walked to the window, was asked to leave my keys and any sharp objects, given a badge, and told to walk through the glass door to the second waiting room. The door buzzed and I was ushered through that room directly to a small courtyard with a clear pathway toward the building. The main door had a big American flag and a decorative plate, to my right was a bigger courtyard with a few parked cars, while to my left was what looked like a storage room next to a flower garden. I walked to the door, to a window with an American soldier sitting inside, who asked me to put up my badge to the window so he could see it. He jotted something down, waited for a few seconds, and then waved to me to go inside as the building's door opened.

Beyond the door was a wide corridor with a small seating area to the right. To the left I saw a few pictures of what looked like US officials. I moved closer and I saw a recognizable face – the Ambassador from the other day. Next to him was US President Nixon, but I didn't recognize the third person, so I moved closer to read his name.

"*That's Kissinger,*" a voice said.

I turned around to see someone roughly my age, wearing a neat shirt and tie. "*Mr Robert?*" I asked.

"*Call me Bob. How are ya?*" he replied, while indicating I should walk with him through the door at the end of the corridor.

"*I am very well, Mr Bob, thank you.*"

"*Just Bob,*" he said. "*Sit down,*" adding, "*these are your papers?*"

"*Yes, sir... Bob.*" as I handed him my file to look through.

"*We follow you on the news. Your English is good. Where did you learn that?*" he asked.

"*I graduated from Sana's University's English department*" I replied, "*but I also like reading English literature, and I also speak some French.*"

He paused, changed his seating position to be more upright and looked at me. "*French? How is that?*"

"*I learnt French when I was a child in Djibouti, but I already forgot most of it. I still remember some of it, which helped me in learning English,*" I replied.

"*You continue to impress, Abdulaziz,*" said Robert. "*Now tell me this, do you want to study in the States so you can learn new skills?*"

"*Yes, of course,*" I replied.

"*So we'll send you to the States to study there with a fully funded Fulbright scholarship. Here ... fill in this form and have a look at this brochure. I'll be right back,*" Robert said before leaving the room.

So, I am going to America after all, I thought to myself. I filled in various sections of the form – personal information, educational background, work history – and was asked to name and rank what I would like to study and in which Universities. I wasn't sure. I hadn't thought this far yet. Did I want to go to New York? Maybe I could work there while studying and make some money. Would I get a student allowance? And how much would it be? And can I bring my family? So many questions. I finished filling in the form, leaving some gaps, and kept wondering to myself. *Maybe I can study law, or economics. Maybe I should pursue journalism to be a professional journalist who develops stories as opposed to just editing and broadcasting. Maybe...*

"*You're done?*" asked Bob, as he walked into the room with a huge file.

"*Some parts are still missing. I'm not sure what to put,*" I replied.

"*Show me.*" He took the form and started going through it. "*Oh, you're married and have two kids. Okay, Does your wife work?*"

"*No,*" I replied, "*but she is in University.*"

"*That's good,*" he said, pausing for a second as he finished going through the form. "*Now pay attention, you want to pick an area in which the degree will help you in any career area, and you want to pick a University that is easy to get into and in a place that isn't expensive to live in. You have a family to look after.*

"*I advise you to go for Masters in English or in Public Administration. We'll add in a letter of recommendation and send it to a few Universities where cost of living isn't high. Let's see what goes through and I'll call you as soon as we hear back. Any questions?*"

I had many questions in my mind. Like *What exactly does a Master of Public Administration entail? When will I hear back? Why did you pick me in the first place? What is life in America like?* and many others, but instead, I said "*No, thank you, Bob.*"

We shook hands, and then I left and went to work. It looked like the family was still in the Embassy's waiting area. I waved goodbye but they didn't see me.

I asked myself where I could find information about America. There were no public libraries in Yemen, the university library was a sad sight, at best, and most of the materials in the library were in Arabic anyway as they were recycled from Egypt or gifted from Arab libraries. Even newsstands had meager collections. It felt like America was a faraway planet – we know it exists, but very little beyond that. In fact, everywhere was a faraway planet when you were in Yemen.

It had occurred to me that on a slow news day they would use international news as a filler, and I wondered about the news services that sent us such materials. Perhaps I could find the source and through it some additional information about the United States, and draw a more complete picture in my mind beyond the occasional item about the war in Vietnam.

I arrived at the office around noon and started my usual routine at the newsroom, keeping an eye on who's who in the office and keeping an ear out in case there was any discussion of international news. One journalist specialized in international news. He received wires and cables from the Middle East News Agency based in Cairo that included regional and international news, and then he rewrote it for the Yemeni audience. Perhaps rewrote was a misnomer; he basically copied it.

"*Haitham, I'm going to the cafeteria to get some tea, do you want anything?*" I asked him.

"*Wait, I'm coming with you,*" he replied.

As we walked down the stairs, he asked me, "*How is work? It must be exhausting to be working late all the time.*"

"*Yeah. Making a living. The head producer promised to hire someone to help,*" I replied

"*Be careful, he might hire his nephew again. He's been trying to find him a job here for a while now. His nephew is a deadbeat ... very lazy,*" Haitham said

It was curious how someone who barely copied a couple of news items a day described someone else as being very lazy. Haitham's own work could be done in less than an hour but took him all day.

"*I don't know him,*" I said. "*How is it working with you? A lot of international news?*"

He took a deep sip of his tea and stared into the distance – like a visionary about to impart some words of wisdom – and exhaled an orphan, "*Yeah...*"

Took me aback. I wasn't sure if he was pulling my leg, but he seemed serious, so, I asked him, "*I'm thinking of including something international in the English news as well. Where do you get the international news from? It's not on the blackboard.*"

"*Come, I'll show you,*" he said as we walked back upstairs. "*The cables come every day and we put them in this black folder, organized by date. Usually from Cairo but sometimes from other places like Beirut. Lately we've been getting some from Saudi Arabia, you know, about Hajj and stuff,*" Haitham said.

Bingo, I thought to myself. *I can skim through them tonight when most are gone and see what comes out.* But as I saw the folder, I thought it was rather light. There had to be much more than this, so I asked him about that.

"*We put the old ones in the Archives, down the hall next to the toilets,*" Haitham explained.

Good to know, I thought to myself.

The next day was Friday, the weekend. When I woke up, I told Aziza about my previous day in the embassy, telling her about the scholarships and prospects. I told her that I had filled in the application and was hoping to pursue a Master's degree in America, but that it wasn't a done deal yet. It was only the beginning and might or might not happen.

"*I don't like this, I hope it doesn't happen,*" she said grudgingly.

Chapter 2: Origins

Aziza was uncomfortable with these quickly unfolding plans. Nobody likes change, especially when it comes at a time of uncertainty. I was only starting my career and it was a good government job with benefits. We had many bills to pay, two children, and my father wanted me to help him get married.

Aziza had overheard that my father came to Sana'a to ask for my help to get married. She had taken the opportunity and asked him to accompany her to the clinic when they would administer the kids' vaccines. Apparently, although the father was required, he could be replaced by the grandfather, as in many families the primary breadwinner was a migrant in Saudi Arabia or elsewhere. Aziza had been keen to do this quickly, as it gave her a chance to hear from him about his marriage, particularly, about his bride-to-be.

This was news to me. I know Aziza was a shrewd woman and could get things done, but hitting two birds with one stone was impressive. I was anxious to get a heads-up of what she had learnt, and her position on it. After all, I don't want to commit anything to my father without her blessing first, as chances are it would come back to haunt me.

So I sat up, and said, "*You dangerous woman, what did you find out?*"

"*It's Ghaya, daughter of Abdullah Muhsen. Their house is next to your grandfather's sorghum field... I hate her*"

"*Wow, okay. Maybe that's why he's proud of his sorghum crop this year. How did they meet?*" I asked.

"*He was probably working in the field or something, and she probably walked by, presenting herself,*" she said. "*That bitch.*"

I smiled and lay back and said, "*That's probably how we met.*" Next thing I know was SMACK.

Yeah. I deserved that smack. The truth of the story is that once I knew there was a girl in the village named Aziza, I thought she was the one for me, and the proof was in the name! Abdulaziz and Aziza. So I had to get to know her and propose. Getting married was a rite of passage for any young man, myself included.

Let me share the story of how my mother and father met.

Sins of the Father: Yaseen's Story

Deep in the mountains of rural Yemen at the turn of the 20th century, my father was the first-born son of a feudalist landlord. My grandfather, Ahmed, was happy that his first born was a boy and called him Yaseen, which also means *blessed*. My grandfather was so happy that he assigned a cow for my father, so that its milk would help him grow strong bones. A dedicated cow was a big deal.

My grandfather's lands were around an off-shoot village away from the nearest settlement where most of our family lived. The village was a few houses on a hilltop with spectacular views of the area around it, surrounded by mostly arid lands bordering a small valley. My grandfather was determined to convert every inch of the rocky area into cultivatable agricultural land that the villagers could use. He did that through dynamite he bought from Aden when it was a British colony, and, through dedicated and hard work, proved you could be somewhat successful, so long you put in enough work and suffering into it.

My grandfather was a very demanding and hard-headed guy, but he was also very generous. They dubbed him Ahmed Qouroush, as Qouroush is the plural of Qirsh, which means *coin*, referring to his wealth. My grandfather would grow obsessed with any project until he had seen it through. He had the biggest house in the area with three floors: the ground floor was for livestock, the second was the reception area where guests would come as well as a guest bedroom that my older aunts usually occupied, the third floor was the bedrooms, and the kitchen was on the rooftop. The view from the roof was spectacular, spanning across the valley to the other hills. Perfect place for an early morning tea.

My father had different problems during his childhood. My grandfather would force him to hike some twelve miles across the valley to learn Quran and literacy at the hands of a Sheikh in the main settlement. The valley had much more greenery and we had many family members there, including some of my grandfather's cousins. The reason my grandfather moved to his arid hill was because of a disagreement with his family, and his hard work in improving the land was traceable to his personal vendetta against his family, determined to show them he was doing better than they were. The usual story of men with big egos.

When he was ten years old, my father, Yaseen, had to develop his workmanship skills, and proved to be quite a talented bricklayer. He would take the leftover stones blasted by dynamite and build terraces or make-shift shelters for animals. My grandfather made good use of my father's talents as he was strategic about placing the dynamite sticks and developed some expertise in using them. Soon enough, there was a stone-laid road in our tiny village, and my father was starting to work on his own house just a stone's throw away from my grandfather's.

When he was seventeen years old, my father married his first wife, Aisha. She bore him two daughters. They were both named by my grandfather, as was the habit. The first was named Hadiya, meaning *the gift*, and the second followed a year later, and was named Nooria, meaning *the light*. It is no surprise that my grandfather, and my father Yaseen, were hoping for boys; they wanted to expand the family presence in the area and populate our little village. Unfortunately, Aisha passed away just a day after giving birth to the second child, leaving my teenage father a broken man with two infant girls on his hands.

It was a traumatic experience for him, not only losing his young wife and moving back into his father's house, but having to care for his two infant daughters. Luckily, his aunts stepped in and took over raising the two girls. They always scolded Yaseen for not being able to provide much, independent of his father, that they would find him a new wife to look after the girls, that he should have at least had a son. Yaseen didn't see himself taking more of this, and decided to leave everything and everyone, and moved to Aden.

Aden was a great city of the British empire and one of the world's busiest ports at the time, ranking next to New York and Liverpool. There were many stories about Aden, the hustle and bustle, the royal navy and huge commercial boats, the numerous languages and communities, and the unmistakable charm of a port city. Yaseen was set to carve a future for himself there and make a fresh start. It is the place where dynamite comes from, after all.

The day my father arrived in Aden, he was hired as a coolie laborer, carrying big bags of merchandise onto and off boats. He was very impressed by how much money he could make from a day's work, noting that he was rarely, if ever, paid by his father. It was, however, the lowest-paid job in the city. None of the workers needed any identification or papers; all they had to do was just show up and carry, and then get paid at the end of the day. The extent of the commerce in the port almost guaranteed that anyone would get work as a coolie laborer.

After a short while, several tradesmen began to ask Yaseen to show up at specific dates and times and gave him extra pay after seeing how well-built he was and that he was capable of loading more than most laborers. He made good money over two years of working in the port, and for the first time, he sent some money back home, along with clothes and toys for his two daughters. Being alone in a new city, starting fresh, was exciting, yet it reminded him of what he left back home. Perhaps sending back was one way of dealing with his past – a past that included a dedicated milk cow, long hikes on rough terrain, and the strenuous work as a bricklayer that contributed to his current success in Aden. Yaseen was often keen to ask what was being loaded. Was it foodstuff for the troops? Spices from India? Garments from the UK? Ivory and hide from Africa? So many things were coming and going to and from so many places.

Yaseen was a curious and rebellious man. He wanted to visit these places, learn more about the world. He had so many plans but was torn between staying close to home and establishing a new life in Aden, or crossing the ocean to the lands of garments and hides and exploring the world. He had friends on one of the ships that often shuffled back and forth from the port city of Djibouti just across the Gulf of Aden, and considered making the trip. He could be back within a week and wouldn't miss that much pay. It was receiving a letter from his father asking him to come home that tipped the scales in favor of making that trip. He didn't want to go home, and he definitely did not want to work for his father again. Aden had been good to him, and he wasn't ready to let it go.

The trip to Djibouti and across the sea was an eye-opener for him. The wide-open blue water with no land in sight was an experience like no other. It was an opportunity to learn about trade, see what was bought and sold, learn how business was conducted, and visit other parts of the world where the merchandise was coming from. Yaseen was intrigued by Djibouti, and although it was a smaller port city than Aden, his pay was better. It helped that experience in Aden was seen as a big plus for merchants, and he found himself telling them his impressions of what was traded, their prices and premiums, and how the market conducts itself. He was a nobody in Aden, but in Djibouti he was a "trade professional" with international experience. He was particularly keen on learning what goods were sold or bartered at a premium in Djibouti, thinking perhaps he could make some serious money engaging in trade.

Yaseen made up his mind. He would go back to Aden only to prepare for a permanent move to Djibouti. After more than two years working in Aden's port, this time he would spend much more time purposefully scouting the markets, learning more about the prices, the inventory, trade activity, and who was who. He needed this knowledge to present himself as the expert he could claim to be in Djibouti, and for that he needed to do his research and study to back up his claims. His plan was to spend whatever savings he had to buy goods and merchandise from Aden that he could sell to traders in Djibouti and vice versa. This way he would have repeat customers and could promise them more merchandise based on their needs and his knowledge of the Aden port activity and markets. Yaseen was eager to make the jump from a coolie laborer to becoming a businessman in his own right.

Yaseen picked a variety of items from Aden to test how they would do. He negotiated hard to get good deals. He was keen on diversifying what he had, to see what would sell and then focus on that. He bade farewell to his friends and fellow coolie laborers and was determined to make a second fresh start in Djibouti.

Upon arrival, he made several rounds of the Yemeni and Arab business community in Djibouti, making introductions and connecting socially. He understood that surviving this business depended on who you knew, who trusted you, and building business relationships. He often made-up stories about his products: These textiles were made in China by the hands of such-and-such communities, who have a secret method of processing the fabrics and giving them colors, and so on. These stories went a long way in facilitating sales. He had a natural knack for it, too.

Yaseen quickly understood that this was most effective on products that targeted women. Women's dresses, make-up, and accessories were a particularly successful business with high margins, as less attention was given to the price and more to the story and design. And it became his specialty. He even become known, by name, to Jawhara, the daughter of one of Djibouti's wealthier Yemeni merchants who ran her father's store. She actually sent to him asking that the next time he had new merchandise, he should come see her first.

Yaseen's business started thriving. He converted most of his living quarters into a storage area, and people started to knock on his door asking to buy some items. Yaseen decided to open a small shop in the main street, a place where he could retail most of his imports instead of selling them to retailers, this way increasing his profits. This would also give him a cover to sell directly to his clientele, but, more importantly, to have a place that Jawhara could visit and where they could converse, away from the prying eyes in her father's shop.

Yaseen was onto something. He was impressed by Jawhara, who was not only wealthy, well educated, and shrewd, but also spectacularly beautiful. Even her name, Jawhara, is Arabic for *jewel*. She had rejected many previous offers of marriage from a number of Yemeni merchants and Djiboutian dignitaries. She saw herself an equal – if not more – and not just someone's wife. Yaseen was quite keen on buying merchandise that spoke to Jawhara's taste and style preferences, and she grew to become his biggest buyer, with many of his items sitting on her shelves and not his, while he made trips to Aden to find more goods to buy, scouting its market and harassing its retailers for his unique merchandise requests.

Yaseen couldn't stop thinking about Jawhara. She seemed too good for him and was in the upper echelons of society while he was a newcomer to town. He needed to find a way to impress her, beyond his salesman charm and his well-built physique. He had to find a way to win her heart. During one of his tours to Aden, he found what he was looking for – a pair of silver slippers that looked magical. They were spectacular, the slippers had topaz and turquoise stones on the strap, white leather as the base, and were covered with silver on all sides. They were like nothing else he'd ever seen, and, despite costing him a small fortune, he was sure they would melt Jawaher's heart.

Yaseen prepared his little store for Jawaher's visit next week to look at his merchandise as usual. This time he even added some decorations and prepared the place for a Cinderella-story proposal, using the silver shoes this time, instead of the customary ring. After all, women do love their slippers, especially silver ones.

I never really understood what my mother saw in my father. She was the daughter of a wealthy merchant in the thriving port of Djibouti who had the world in her palm; he was a bricklayer-turned-salesman with eccentric styling. Perhaps it was the shallow charisma women seem to fall for. And of course, silver slippers.

Jawhara was impressed with Yaseen's proposal, but she laid out one condition. She asked him to sell his shop and work for her in her shop. She wanted to capitalize on his skills and literally cut out the middleman, and put more resources in his hands so that he could do trade on behalf of her shop. She was a businesswoman after all, and I suppose she saw potential. Yaseen was quick to accept. The wedding was legendary, it was the talk of the town for a month, particularly the slippers she wore.

A year later, I was born. My father Yaseen continued with his trips to Aden, but also started making trips inland on the railway into the Ethiopian heartland. Emperor Selassie of Ethiopia was particularly welcoming of Yemeni traders, and Yaseen found many trade and barter opportunities, buying hides, leather products, and all sorts of goods and handicrafts for which he could charge a significant premium in Aden. Yaseen came up with the idea of opening and financing an off-shoot megastore in Dire Dawa in Ethiopia, with the idea of serving as a trade choke point. This megastore became a stopover-turned-destination for reluctant businessmen who wanted to go to Ethiopia and bring in more goods, and slowly became the monopoly chokepoint it was intended to be.

That venture kept my father busy and away for prolonged periods of time in my early years. Home had become more of a transit location for him. At first, I didn't mind as I would spend most of my time in the shop with my mother and grandfather. I always preferred to stand around the entrance looking at the street and the people and carts moving, with the strong smell of spices engraved in my memory. Every time I find myself in a spice shop, my memories take me back to those early days.

My mother was the oldest of four. However, with time, her siblings wanted more to do with their father's business, especially after my ailing grandfather passed away. My mother always expressed her disappointment in her siblings, as they didn't pay much attention to the Dire Dawa operation, and their in-fighting started to harm the business. She hoped that they would become more mature, unfortunately, getting older only increased the in-fighting.

It was a literal crossroad: she needed to salvage what she could from the shop, and she saw some merit in moving to Dire Dawa and taking her inheritance with her. It was also an escape from Djibouti in a sense. The city she had grown up in as its darling princess has become a different place. There were too many strangers now, and the family's prominence had dwindled, and the simple life was no longer as simple. A fresh start would be welcome.

Yaseen loved Dire Dawa too, as it gave him more prominence than Djibouti ever had. He was running the biggest business in this small town and established significant social influence and following. The shop was the biggest and most modern shop in the town, with its own power generator for electricity, and on the second floor was their residence. Yaseen would turn on the lights at night and keep a radio running for people to gather, socialize, and mingle.

People would hang out around the shop just for the sake of it, and he found himself offering tea and sometimes snacks, which catered to his ego as a generous host. This shop had almost become the town's square. People would come to him with their problems, happy to listen to his stories about the port of Djibouti and the great port of Aden, and ask him to show them what he bought from recent traders who came to the town. I see now why he spent so much of his time hanging around the shop in Dire Dawa.

With my mother's arrival, things started to change. She was, after all, his boss and the owner of the shop. One of the first things she did was to reorganize the shop and inventory what it had. To her surprise, the shop wasn't only unprofitable, but it had serious liquidity problems due to Yaseen's barter system, building an inventory of "crap" that nobody in Dire Dawa wanted. Very few people could afford the accessories and luxuries Yaseen had in the shop. This wasn't the port of Aden under the British administration or Djibouti under the French mandate. This was a small town in rural Ethiopia where people had very little discretionary income.

My mother was from the Jeddawi family, tracing their origins to the city of Jeddah in Saudi Arabia. Her father moved to Djibouti following the declaration of the Arab Revolt in Jeddah and sought a fresh start in Djibouti after wandering around the Red Sea. She had heard stories about the old days in Jeddah and the news of family members who remained there; how they dealt with the Ottomans and the Sharifians, and then the Al-Saud; and others who moved to Egypt, the Levent, and places as far as Zanzibar. They were natural businesspeople with good money sense running in their veins, and Jawhara was no exception.

Jawhara prepared Yaseen to go on a business trip. She asked him to take the expensive "crap" merchandise and sell it in Djibouti or Aden, and come back with cash only so that they could start again using the old and proven business model. It seemed that Yaseen belonged on the road, traveling from one port to another, visiting markets and vendors across the Gulf of Aden. These were familiar grounds to him, and I was increasingly curious about going to Aden and Yemen, my home to which I had never been.

I went to a French-language school in Dire Dawa, on my mom's insistence. She was fluent in Arabic and French, and spoke some Somali, Amharic, and even Italian. Running her father's shop, she had had to speak whatever her customers spoke so she could deliver good customer service, and she was keen on me building some of these skills. She told me that had my father spoken more languages, he would have been able to travel further and see the world. I didn't like speaking French and all the rules it had; I had no idea how speaking a different language would open doors to that language's world.

Meanwhile, my mother was able to turn the business around, even expanding it, establishing a stand-alone tea shop attached to it so that loitering guests became paying customers. She also built an adjunct house and hostel for travelers next to it as more commerce flocked through Dire Dawa. After school I would work in the tea shop, serving the patrons tea, fried snacks, and sandwiches. I also started learning how to cook basic recipes to feed weary travelers. I remember getting tips from customers, although that was very rare.

In one of his trips to Aden, Yaseen received an urgent letter from his father asking him to return to the village due to his father's ailing health. Yaseen managed to go back to the village and visit his family, including his two daughters. He told his father about everything he had been doing, about Jawhara and me. His daughters were already young women, raised without knowing either their father or mother. It was a bizarre family reunion, with the long-lost son returning home. Although it had only been a decade, the village had changed a lot. There were now a dozen or more houses, the tiny road had been widened to allow trucks to go over it, and the small shrubs he helped plant were now big trees. He had a hard time recognizing many of his family members, meeting their families and learning about their stories, while he told them his story, including his young family in Dire Dawa.

My father's last trip to Yemen changed him, and our little family wasn't sure what came next for us. My mother has become a big employer in the area with much influence. My father increasingly saw himself isolated, unhappy, and torn. He told my mother about going to Yemen, and that he had two daughters from a previous marriage. He told her about his village and family, and all the fortunes they had there. She was visibly upset that he had hidden the secret of his daughters from her the whole time, and not only that, worried her that he had simply abandoned two little girls to grow up motherless and fatherless, and she asked herself what kind of man he really was. It was just too much for her to take in.

"*I want to meet them. Take me to Yemen,*" my mother demanded of my father.

She knew what was going on. He had been generally unhappy, and now he wanted to move back to Yemen where he would be in his element. He was the oldest son and expected to take over from his ailing father. She wanted to see for herself, without trusting his words alone. Perhaps she knew that Yaseen was in constant search for a new start. He wasn't 40 yet and already had three fresh starts - Aden, Djibouti, and Dire Dawa - and now he wanted to move back to where it all started for a fourth start.

When I was ten years old, we moved back to Yemen. My grandfather, Ahmed Qouroush, had given away much of the land he improved and owned, so he grew poorer as a result of reduced rents and lower incomes from fewer yields. When we returned, my father was keen to turn the situation around and become the anchor of the family, focusing on cultivating existing lands and maximizing yields. It was a struggle, to say the least. My father was no farmer; he was a merchant. A remote village is no place for a merchant to be. My mother saw that clearly, and she told him she isn't staying in this village in the middle of nowhere, especially as her quality of life was much better in Dire Dawa.

This is where my parents parted ways. My father felt a stronger obligation to his father's legacy and estate, and the two daughters he had neglected for most of their lives. He told my mother that if she had to leave, she would leave on her own and without me. I am sure that was a hard decision for her to make. It was a painful situation for all of us. I had just turned twelve, and now had a part-time father, and a mother overseas. She promised to visit, and we promised each other to write regularly. I thought family was supposed to give strength to people, but it was always breaking apart. There was nobody out there for me but me.

Growing into My Own

After my mother left, I grew somewhat closer to my older half-sisters. They were curious about me, being the new thing around. They asked about my upbringing, life in the horn, and my weird accent and French. It took some time for me to grow into the family and shake off the feeling of being an adopted child. My father took me to the newly built school a few miles away, they were puzzled at which grade to place me in. They put me straight into grade 5, taking into account my age and my prior education, and I was the youngest in my class.

My teenage years were split between going to school and working on the land. It also gave me some time to get to know my extended family and neighbors. I learnt about Aziza through my older sisters. Perhaps my fascination with her was inherent in mirroring my own name. Her father was an immigrant contractor working in Saudi Arabia, and they lived actually a few houses away, separated by a natural rainwater drainage area that used to get flooded once a year. I asked my grandfather to give me the land where the water drained and the animal barn that came with it, saying I want to make a small plot out of it. He told me that this was a foolish and bad idea, as no matter how strong the terrain and wall I build to contain the soil, the annual rains would drain it away. *Isn't that exactly what you've been doing your whole life*, I wanted to ask him, but didn't want to argue. It wasn't the plot of land I was after; it was the neighbor.

My first attempts in fixing the soil were futile. Every time I lined up the rocks, mudded them well, and ensured there was a big fortified terrace to develop a small plot, it didn't last long. At one point, I saw an older man working on my land plot, trying to rework the stones, so I hurried up to see what was going on.

"*Hey... this is my land,*" I started charging.

"*Abdulaziz, I'm your Uncle Mohammed...*" he said with a firm but kind tone. "*Listen, you can't fight nature, you have to go with nature. When the water flows there is no power that can stop it, what you need to do is create a pathway for the water to flow through and around your plot.*"

He was Aziza's father, returning from one of his trips, and I was a bit rude to him in our first encounter. Speaking of starting off on the wrong foot. I however asked him for help on how to do that. He had worked in construction in Saudi Arabia for many years, and was witness to some impressive projects from which he learnt a few things. He advised me on how to first create a small water barrier a little bit uphill to break the force, then another one, then create a small pool that overflowed into a canal-type water drainage system. It was an interesting thought process, and it worked. We sort-of bonded over this project, and I was glad we did.

He would stay for a few weeks every year in the village, usually around holidays. Soon I had finished another four years of schooling and completed primary education until grade 9, which was the end of the road for most people. I was keen to take my newfound experience and build a few more agricultural plots in the village. And then a letter from my mother arrived. She asked me to go join her in Dire Dawa and continue my education there.

I felt that I was always an outcast. Although I was born in Djibouti, I was not a Djiboutian; I didn't belong to Dire Dawa, and only now was able to establish some friendships here. I replied to my mother that I wanted to stay in Yemen, I had already fixed a bit of land and wanted to do more, and that I wanted to marry Aziza.

It was a bold move for me. I had been quite upset about her leaving us. I knew that my father wasn't particularly pleasant and had been troublesome, but what about me? Was I just another write-off, left to pursue my own path to wherever that might lead me? The current arrangement might have been be far from ideal for both of us, but at the end of the day, we both needed to make our own decisions.

Still, truth be told, I was always broke. I didn't have much income apart from the little handouts my grandfather gave me or from working on peoples' lands. And I wanted to build my own house, get married, and become something. So I went to my grandfather and asked him for help. His words kept resonating in my mind.

He said, "*Abdulaziz... Son... Back in the day I used to be Ahmed Qouroush. Now, I am only Ahmed Paisa* [meaning worth only a single penny]. *I tell you what, demolish that small animal hut in your plot, and see if you can reuse the rocks and materials. May God be with you.*"

I kissed him on the forehead and left him. I promised myself that this would never be me. I would be rich. I must be rich. I was not going to build a home out of an animal hut. I had to get out of there.

In the earlier days, opportunities for work were concentrated in Aden, but now, as the British are leaving, opportunities became progressively rarer. I decided to go to Taiz city, the second biggest city in the country and a few hours' drive from the village. I would hitch a ride there, and find work – any type of work. I asked my father to look after my plot of land and went to Taiz.

Chapter 3: Taiz City

Taiz City had a special air to it. It sat on a mountain side overlooking many valleys. It had a sloped topography that needed getting used to, where you were probably going either up or down most of the time. But among my main discoveries was the complex systems of mini-dams and rainwater runoff cisterns it used to manage water overflow and preserve it for use in dry seasons. This engineering complexity resonated with me, seeing the wonders that man could use to tame nature.

Upon arriving in Taiz, I stayed at a common rest house in a neighborhood called Moses' Gate at the western entrance of the city. It was a usual place for travelers, on one hand being away from the private quarters of the city's residents, and on the other hand being close to a major water catchment public works project that needed many laborers. It was known as Camp Kennedy by its American sponsors, or just "the Camp" by everybody else. Naturally, the presence of work meant that many migrant workers stayed near the area. The work wasn't too bad. New guys like me were given simple stone-laying tasks so the contractors could observe, then decide if we are going to be given other, more-demanding tasks or not. It was my first ever job and daily wage. Plus the irony of crossing the rainwater runoff cisterns to Moses' Gate wasn't lost on me. Maybe Taiz was my promised land.

This community of migrants had a lot in common. Most of us were more or less in the same age group; many were working to save money or send it back to their families. Hopes and dreams were a common driver, and some saw it as a stop-over in a longer journey to Sana'a. Many unfamiliar faces quickly become familiar with the dreams and toil connecting us. Once, as I was scanning these faces, I once saw familiar a face at the rest house; Anees, a classmate from my primary school, had come to drop a parcel to a traveler going back to their village. I was thrilled to see Anees and catch up with him.

"*Hey Anees,*" I waved. "*How are you? How long have you been in Taiz?*"

"*Since school finished, I came to Taiz to register for high school, and I also work here at my uncle's restaurant. You should come by and meet my uncle,*" Anees replied.

"*Yes, we should catch up. If anyone else from our class is here that you know, we should arrange a get together.*"

That weekend, I went to see Anees at his uncle's restaurant, which was one of the larger ones in town. His uncle was an aged person and he had been working in that restaurant for many years, and it continued to expand on and on. His uncle waved from afar and signaled us both to come toward him. I followed Anees and shook hands with his uncle. His hand was remarkably soft, especially compared to my hand which was rough from carrying rocks and hauling wheelbarrows for the last couple of months.

"*When did you arrive?*" he asked.

"*I just arrived earlier this summer,*" I replied.

Then he signaled to Anees to go organize the fresh produce being offloaded to the restaurant, perhaps a diversion to ask me a few questions

"*Whose son are you? Who are your family?*" he further asked.

"*I'm a Saqqaf from AlHadharim village, in Adeem valley.*"

Then he interrupted me asking, "*What relation is Ahmed Qouroush to you?*" referring to my late grandfather.

"*He was my grandfather,*" I replied.

"*Ah really? Good man, God rest his soul. He always used to come eat here you know,*" he said, adding "*So what are you doing in Taiz, young man?*"

"*For work. I'm working. At the Camp,*" I replied.

He looked at me with a look of pity and said, "*No, don't work in the Camp. That is dangerous work for someone like you. You should go to school. Tomorrow you go with Anees to school, and I will give you work here. You will take over the dough from Anees, and you'll work on it in the morning before school. Do you know how to make dough?*"

He didn't give me a chance to say yes or no. He looked adamant on what I should do and didn't give me an option otherwise. It was true, I would prefer to work with someone who seemed keen for my wellbeing and close to a familiar person. Working indoors beat working in the sun and the uncertainty of being a daily laborer.

Things started moving well with school and work. My hands were getting softer as I worked the oiled dough and prepared all types of bread and delicacies. One type that seemed to be a bestseller was sugary fried dough known as *Ushaar*, which was a calorie-heavy breakfast staple for most workers, taken with a glass of sugary red tea. We easily sold hundreds of these every day. I prepared the dough from the previous night, and started frying and piling up Ushaar before going to school. We often hitched a ride on the back of a pickup truck to school, and I mastered the art of jumping off a moving vehicle and landing on my feet. Life looked good. For a while.

Then Anees and I had a falling out. It was his uncle's restaurant, and his uncle was always a bit tougher on him, especially when it came to buying the food supplies, inspecting their quality, and dealing with vendors. Every time the tomatoes were sub-par or we ran low on meat, it was Anees's fault. His uncle was growing impatient with him, and used to threaten him with me taking over his job. *"Look at Abdulaziz... He knows how to work like people are supposed to,"* his uncle would say. This was driving a wedge between Anees and me. I saw it in Anees's face. Competition was not welcome, especially from me.

Managing conflict wasn't my forte, especially during my youth. It was nice to be praised, getting positive reinforcement for diligent and hard work. It is true that I didn't have the management responsibilities that Anees had, especially when dealing with suppliers who took him for granted given his young age. Perhaps I contributed to Anees's feelings of isolation and competitiveness; a year's worth of working and staying together had piled up many tensions.

One day, Anees sabotaged the dough. He added salt and something sour that I couldn't make out. I know it was him, but I didn't want to escalate. I told his uncle so, thanked him for a year's work and experience, and quit my job, telling him I should move on. I even had some pay due for me which I didn't collect and left it to compensate him for the wasted dough. As I was walking out, picking up my plastic shopping bag with a few personal items, I saw Anees beaming at me.

"That's messed up, man. Accusing me? May God open doors of promise for you and for me." I told him with a sorrow in my voice

that losing a brother and a friend was far worse than losing a job, especially in this town of strangers.

"*It's not me, it is you. Or you don't think you make mistakes?*" Anees shrugged me off.

"*My mistakes seem to make you happy.*" I replied.

He stepped back, picked up a mango from the produce stock box, threw it at me, and walked away. Perhaps it was a parting gift or an attempt to side-step the issue. I put the mango in my plastic bag and left, unsure where to go, until I found myself back at the rest house at Moses' Gate, the place where I had seen Anees for the first time in what felt like too long ago. I was easily replaceable. I also felt that his uncle was relieved that I left as he didn't try to keep me. He probably saw the tensions building; tensions that he repeatedly inflamed.

I must admit that had it not been for Anees's uncle, I wouldn't have continued with high school. I felt somewhat academically superior to others; perhaps it was my Dire Dawa education that gave me a leg up among my peers. But I needed to make money and build my life. Maybe this education thing could wait, as they didn't hire part-timers at the Camp.

But this time around, the Camp felt like a strange place. They were hiring fewer hands and with the abundance of fresh muscle, the contractors got to pick and choose. After a few days of work, it looked like I didn't make the cut to move to better work within the Camp, and the contractor in charge mocked my soft palms. I was torn between continuing at the Camp as it was more or less the sole recruiter in town, returning to Anees's uncle and trying to work something out and also continue my studies, or travel elsewhere. Maybe the capital city Sana'a would be more promising. I'd been hearing a lot about people who went to Sana'a, and I thought I could make enough money to marry Aziza and make a better life. But for now, being a bricklayer must do.

My thoughts were interrupted by a familiar voice calling my name. It was Anees. Maybe this was the answer I'd been waiting for.

"*Abdulaziz... This letter came for you,*" he said.

It was a letter from my mother. I had written to tell her about my work and studies, knowing she would be happy to know what I'm doing and my progress at school. Anees looked at me with great curiosity about the letter, I looked at him and told him it was a letter from my mom, and thanked him for delivering it.

"*It was my uncle who ruined the dough,*" he told me as he was leaving.

I nodded, implying, *okay, I'll pretend that I believe you,* and watched him as he left the rest house. I couldn't wait to read this letter from my mom. I missed her dearly in this harsh world. My mother was ecstatic about my plans, saying that I inherited my pursuit of education from her side of the family. She encouraged me to focus on my studies and not let work distract me, and she sent me a good chunk of money, and said she would continue to send more.

It was funny that just ten minutes ago I thought that my predicament could be solved by begging for my job back from Anees's uncle, or by giving up on school. Now Anees said it was his uncle who wanted me out, and that was probably true. Business has been tough lately with more competition opening up, and he probably couldn't justify two part-time young people who aren't available during the peak hours of breakfast and lunch. The dough was Anees's job before I came in, after all. But my bigger problem was what to tell my mom regarding losing my job, or suspending my studies for now. I decided the next day to skip work and go to the high school instead, at least this way I could tell her that I was at school earlier today when I wrote a reply, and delay sharing the bad news for now. Maybe by tomorrow I'd figure something out. I also took the time to see how much these shillings my mom sent were actually worth in local currency.

My school looked very different at sunrise. It was a ghostly building that came to life slowly, first with the resident guard, who lived with his wife and kids in a small room by the main entrance, opening the main gate and dusting the access paths, followed by spraying water over them ahead of many stomping feet. Then I saw a cart vendor coming by to sell some snacks for the students as the hustle and bustle started. I had never noticed the cart man as by the time I arrived in the morning rushing to class, he had already sold out and gone. I saw some familiar faces – teachers and students who I recognized by name – and many younger faces flocking in, some lazily gazing into the distance while others carrying determined faces full of purpose.

That is when it hit me. All of these were paying customers, potentially my paying customers. I could set up shop right there, across from the gate, and sell Ushaar and make things work. I know everything about making Ushaar and I felt I could do it if I tried. I couldn't stay in the guest house forever. I had already saved up some money, and now I had a skill. I rented a tiny shop, bought a metal fryer and three small stoves, a few more things and there, my own place of business. Friendship Cafeteria for Ushaar and Tea. The place was small to keep the costs low, plus I also slept there on a make-shift fold-out mattress, cutting the cost of the bed at the rest house and giving me a strong feeling of independence.

Surprisingly, Anees was among my first customers and a key promoter in the school. I owed him an apology for being wrong about him. Perhaps the name 'Friendship' struck a chord, or it was our mutual feelings of guilt where the other was concerned. But it worked and many students passed by to get some Ushaar on their way to class. I was still the last one arriving to class but with much less stress. In no time, Friendship Cafeteria expanded, and we now had several sorts of sandwiches, mango juice and lemonade, as well as a growing menu to keep the regulars happy.

But Aziza was always on my mind. In a couple of years I had become a successful business owner, was finishing high school, and had many dreams to pursue. My aunts would tell me that they found a bride for me, asking me about "my specifications" only to interrupt me with their own descriptions: *She must be gentle and tender yet tough enough to hand-slaughter a goat. She must be fair and tall but know her way around the barn to get work done.* I'm not sure what made me more uncomfortable, them hammering at me for being single at the young but old age of seventeen or them planning my life for me.

Time to make a move. I proposed to Aziza the old fashioned way. No silver slippers here, but I did shower her with gifts. Quantity seemed to compensate for quality. Cupid or not, it was convenient enough to show that we were meant for each other, as old ladies kept trying to marry us all the time. My father was particularly pushing me to get married and settle down, but I think his concern was losing me to the lure of big cities as opposed to having me around. He had his share of adventure and knew how this worked, so why couldn't I have mine.

My experience in Taiz was also an eye opener for me: bigger cities present bigger opportunities and bigger problems too, as I would soon learn. My little business was starting to capture some attention that isn't always wanted, like all the permits I was supposed to apply for, the intensifying competition from cart vendors, and my landlord trying to raise the rent all the time, having seen the foot traffic.

By 1970, I was finishing high school, had a bit of money saved up from my work, and was unsure what to do next. I turned to my mother for advice – advice that changed my life.

My Dear Abdulaziz,
Your father wasted his life and part of mine, and no one ever pities "the gifted one" once they fall from grace. There is a big world for you to pursue with unfulfilled dreams for me and you. Go be the legend your grandfather said you will be.

I wrote back to her saying how hard it was to be on my own, hoping for a more charitable response. I asked her what my maternal grandfather had said about me. She said she would tell me what he used to say and why he named me Abdulaziz when we met. In her letters, she kept asking about Aziza, especially given it had been almost a year since I had proposed and it was customary to have a short engagement period. She said she would come to the village during the next Eid festival, and that I better make arrangements for my wedding then. Mom was right: I had been too preoccupied with the call of the head to heed the call of the heart.

At eighteen, I felt I had already gone through a lot, from my childhood in the horn, my upbringing in rural Taiz, my high school in Taiz city, and now building my family. I'd been on the move for a bit, and it was time I settle down and make a home of my own – my home in Aziza's arms. But it was a difficult decision to make. I still had my room in my grandfather's house, and he did leave me a bit of land and that animal hut before he passed away, suggesting I use its stones to build a home of my own. What I needed was a plan, and I had to take action before the Eid festival was here.

A Family of My Own

It was loud. Very loud. The drumming and the singing were all over the place. It was my mother's doing by paying extra tips to the drummers, as it was a status symbol to keep it running for longer and make a hell of a lot of noise. It was noisy, people coming and going, wishing the bride and groom good fortune, hugs and kisses. It was a small community and my late grandfather was its patriarch in a sense, so coming to my wedding and celebrating with us was obligatory.

Aziza was something else. It was a dark space and sparsely lit. People carried their own lanterns to get around and light the place until we got into the main reception room in my late grandfather's house, where the men gathered around me, as the groom. Next to me stood my father and next to him Aziza's father, and around us was everybody else. Shortly thereafter the Imam came in, and the official ceremony began.

"*Who is the groom?*" The Imam asked.

"*That young lad is,*" someone said.

"*Make space for the Imam,*" my father yelled at the attendees.

"*Come on, make it quick, move... MOVE.*" He continued yelling at the gathering crowd as the loud drumming continued outside.

"*And who is the father of the bride?*" the Imam asked – only to be interrupted again by my father pointing out and saying, "*We already fixed up everything, and everything is agreed on.*"

"*Ya Sheikh Yaseen...*" The Imam replied flattered my father by calling him Sheikh; my father was paying him after all. He added, "*These are nuptials, not a game. Let me do my job.*"

"*Bring some tea for the Imam so that he can pay attention. This is not a game*" my father yelled.

I sort of see the charisma that my mother saw in my father, but I know through first-hand experience that this attitude got old quickly when push came to shove. I was my father's son but I would make the best life I could for Aziza and my new family.

After the nuptials were done, I was taken to the next room to see my bride. It was customary for the groom to congratulate the bride, accompanied by her mother and other women from the family, and give her a gift, in this case, a huge piece of satin fabric. My mother had brought it with her, and, as she opened it, cash fell from within the folds. My mother had her own ways of impressing. After that, everybody else was invited out of the room and it was just the two of us, Aziza and me, for the first night of our lives together.

A few days later, it was time for my mother to return to Dire Dawa. We chatted for a while. She told me about her life and adventures in Dire Dawa and how that city was blossoming. Her business was the first to introduce a TV box in the city, and she used that traffic to expand business further. She also took time to get to know Aziza and encouraged her to pursue education and learning opportunities. She wanted to show Aziza an example of a woman who was strong, independent, and could look after herself.

My mom then told me that she also had plans to visit her ancestral home in Hejaz and perform Hajj pilgrimage in Mecca in the next couple of years or so. She told me stories about how her father left Jeddah at a young age, following the conflict in the 1920s, and how she'd been trying to reconnect with that side of her family. I suppose we're all migrants in this world; we go wherever our feet take us, often tracing back our steps seeking closure and to reconnect with those who we lost. I felt that she left in a hurry, accompanied by her trusty companion Meriam, who was in a sense my mom's best friend. She left me some cash and her gold necklace and told me to sell it if times got hard on my young family. She promised to visit again on her way back from Hejaz, and I looked forward to her new stories of adventure.

Life was good and we were starting to normalize our new life. Aziza encouraged me to build a house in the village – the ultimate dream for any young couple close to their families. She also wanted me to move out of my grandfather's house and away from my two older half-sisters. My grandfather had gifted me that animal barn, and I might as well finish demolishing it and use the full plot to build a decent house with ample room, especially now that Aziza and I were expecting our first child.

"*That part of the plot is sloped, and half of it is the rainfall stream collection area,*" Aziza's father said.

"*But we can build on this side,*" I responded, objecting. "*In Taiz they have this huge Kennedy Camp project where they build around the stream and it works just fine.*" I added.

"*But it will be expensive,*" he added, touting his experience as a contractor.

My mother-in-law saw the tension building and said she would manage the process. Slow and steady, the construction would progress. Thank God she intervened, as I already felt it was me against the world, with too many demands of me. I needed to create a home for my new family; I also needed to make a living. My mother required me to pursue further education, and now this.

Luckily my mother-in-law read my face; she knew how to manage her husband and got the job done.

My focus for now was moving forward on this project, making sure Aziza got the attention she needed as an expecting mother, and preparing a suitable home for our new child. But she wasn't just my adorable child, she was the first grandchild in the family.

Haifa's birth gave me purpose. It is a truly proud moment in a father's life to hold your own child in your hand. You see the world through her pretty eyes; you feel like a new soul is born within you, she is now a part of you. *Dear Haifa, I would change the world for you, but I can't do that while sticking around this village. I must go to Sana'a.*

Chapter 4: Finding Destiny in Sana'a

The road to Sana'a was long, twisty, and rather remarkable. Mountain peaks threw our jam-packed SUV side to side, and there were roadworks and construction crews all the way. After a grueling twelve-hour trip over three segments, I made it to Sana'a, our nation's capital. We arrived at night at an unassuming travelers' station, with many lodges and hotels scattered around it for you to pick from. Sana'a was the destination for many people from across the country. Some, like me, were students; others were migrant workers or civil servants returning from leave, and many were visitors.

People spoke of the grand streets of Sana'a, its tall buildings, and the fortified old city sitting behind tall walls surrounded by a moat on one side and by a huge palace on the other. Such a beautiful place – with beautiful people, I might add. I wrote to Aziza of my impressions. I used to hide my letters to her inside the pages of magazines I bought to send her, as magazines were rarely available outside Sana'a and I wanted Aziza to learn about the big world out there. Plus an orphan love letter sent via the village courier would stir gossip – something I was keen to avoid.

Despite a decade of violence and unrest, the San'ani people remained welcoming and hospitable. I stayed in an area between the University and the old city in a neighborhood called Al-Qaa, previously known as Qaa el-Yahoud, meaning "grounds of the Jews" in recognition of the Jewish community that lived in the area. Rent was cheaper in this area, and I needed to stretch my savings to last as long as possible, especially as I started my classes, and tried to find work, and establish myself.

My first order of business was to visit the newly opened Sana'a University and see what the hype was about. Some students in my high school talked about pursuing studies there, and my mother left me few options but to at least give it a try. The building stood out with many young men roaming around giving it a distinctively different vibe of everything else around. I walked into the office asking for information on how to enroll with my high school credential in hand. The administrator glanced at it and asked me to return the next day at 10am sharp.

"*And wear something nice. It will be an interview,*" he added.

These are the big leagues, I thought to myself, *and I don't have a point of reference to what that may be.* The next day I put on my best shirt, paperwork in hand, and went a full hour early. To my surprise, I wasn't the only one. There were young men from all over the country lining up outside the office in the courtyard. The first order of business was to pick up an enrollment form, fill it in, and submit it at the window, and then wait outside to be called.

There were about fifty of us outside the building, some sitting on bricks, others standing or squatting. You would often see a local passer-by asking what the gathering was about. I saw a shepherd herding his sheep. This was the outskirts of town after all, and so seeing a flock of sheep wasn't unusual. The officer came out of the office announcing some names. I waited my turn. My name wasn't called. I waited more, getting nervous. We found ourselves huddling around the first person to come out of the interview room.

"*What did they ask? Who was there? What happened in there?*"

"*They are from the Ministry; they asked some questions on what you want to study and why. They also asked some high-school level questions too,*" the young man replied.

I can deal with that, I thought to myself, and then I heard my name called next.

"*Abdulaziz Al-Saqqaf, born 24 October 1952?*" one of the three panelists asked.

I nodded in agreement.

"*Abdulaziz, your marks are excellent. We would like to recommend that you pursue University education in Egypt as a part of the Ministry's scholarship program for young achievers. Pick up this dossier and form, fill it in, and compile the needed documents on the list,*" The same panelist added.

I had expected more questions on why I want to study or something to test my skills. I froze in place with a look of bewilderment for a second, to be interrupted by a second panelist. "*Come back next week to meet with the counselor. He will answer any questions you might have and help you along the process,*" he said, adding, "*Mabrouk!*" in a congratulatory tone.

My thoughts were racing. I was less than a week in Sana'a and already opportunities were knocking on my door. Egypt had been instrumental in building this new Yemen; I had Egyptian teachers in my high school in Taiz, and some of the school curricula was borrowed from Egypt. This is a great opportunity, according to everyone.

But I was torn. I had promised myself to be a better husband and father than my father ever was, and I couldn't do that from a different country. I found myself wandering around the University campus with these thoughts in my head, only to be interrupted by a strange voice. I had never heard English spoken with such an accent before. It was coming from the second floor of the building I was wandering around, so I decided to get closer.

It was coming from the smoking area of the faculty room, and I saw a Caucasian man engaging in discussion with what looked like faculty members from Yemen, Egypt, and other countries. He was the one who spoke with that fascinating accent. I wanted that accent. I felt a sense of relief that this would help me make a decision: I would stay in Yemen, I would bring Aziza and Haifa to Sana'a, and I would make a life here without having to travel to Egypt. It was an amazing relief to have the call of the head and the call of the heart align.

I loitered around the area for a bit more, then decided to go back to the registration office asking to meet again with the panelists. As I was going back, it looked like they had concluded the day's business and were about to leave.

"*You are Abdulaziz, right? What's wrong, son?*" said the panelist who invited me to return the next week to meet with the counselor.

"*I would like to sign up for the English-language program here in the University,*" I replied.

"*Don't waste the opportunity to study abroad. Many don't get this opportunity and you are a distinguished student,*" he replied, emphasizing I should reconsider.

"*I can't. I must stay in Yemen,*" I replied.

"*Come,*" he said, as he traced back his steps into the office. "*Fill up this enrollment form, I already signed it, take it to AbdulKarim at the registration desk and tell him to also withdraw your name from the scholarship list."* He paused and then added, *"Are you sure you can't travel?"*

I looked at him, then to the floor, then back to him and nodded.

"This is a good program and you will do well. May God be with you, and if you need anything you can come see me," he said. Little did I know that the person I was speaking with was the Minister of Education, Mr Ahmed Jaber Afif.

I found myself spending more and more time at Sana'a University. The lecture rooms felt homely and we had a mixed cadre of Yemeni, Egyptian, and American volunteer professors and lecturers. My brush with French gave me an edge over my peers, and soon enough I got my first gig through one of the Yemeni professors to develop a lexicon of business words in the local dialects to identify and standardize what they exactly mean. One professor also worked as a part-time translator to several businessmen to assist in international correspondence, but he struggled in ensuring consistency in the Arabic terminology as multiple traders had different names for the same types of materials.

That task entailed learning about the various types of wood Yemen imported, used in construction, manufacturing, and other sectors. When he wrote a request for quotations to be sent via telex to chambers of commerce around the world, he would be sure the request mentioned the right type of wood, its source, chemical treatment, and other specifications so that it matched what the buyer was looking for. One gig led to the next and I found myself using typesetters to type up telex messages, menus, letters, and all sorts of business correspondence in Arabic and in English, thanks to the patience of the clients, my professors, and the American volunteers. It was a lucrative skill that helped me both improve my English, and meet many people, as well as make more money than I would have making Ushaar and selling sandwiches.

Honestly, I hadn't expected that I would be privy to this world of commerce. The promise of Sana'a was indeed true, and Mom was right - languages open horizons and she was pleased to hear about my adventures in Sana'a and the life I was making. Sana'a was working out for me, and the money I was making was enough to sustain a family. I fixed up my residence, bought some more furniture, and established my marital home. All I needed was to bring my family to Sana'a.

The days passed too slowly when I was far away in Sana'a, juggling studies and work. And they passed too quickly when I was in the village with my family. This kept on for a year, and my purpose was to make as much money as possible to send home to finish the construction of our home, which was, at the time, two rooms, an outdoor kitchen, and a toilet and a reception area. That would suffice. Plus, being a stone's throw away from Aziza's parents' home was a big advantage especially, when it came to helping with Haifa. I took the time to contribute to the construction as much as I could every time I was around, to build it with my own two hands. My father was a bricklayer and I had some experience at the Kennedy Camp in Taiz.

But it was hard, and I saw that we used many of the stones from the old barn. However, I took it upon myself to show off my wood knowledge, evaluating the wood to be used in the roofing of my house. Aziza looked more comfortable in the village than she expected to be in Sana'a. It was her first trip outside the village, her accent was a dead giveaway that she was a rural woman from Taiz's villages, and I felt that she was intimidated with moving away and to break into Sana'ani society: she wasn't ready.

But Sana'a was where the future lay. I couldn't keep commuting back and forth over this distance forever, plus I couldn't stay away from Haifa for long, especially now that she waddles around with plans for mischief. The twelve-hour journey from the village to Sana'a could be a demanding one, but it had become routine for me, and I would make plans to rent a car with a driver to take some furniture and wares from Sana'a to the village for our almost-complete house, and bring back my wife and child on the return leg – which was better than the hassle of collective transport. That was the plan, but only the first part would go as intended.

The news was that Aziza was expecting our second child. Walid was born in 1973. And now they are two; I've been blessed twice and most grateful for this gift. This also meant that I had to focus on getting serious about my work and career. I was already halfway through completing my bachelor's degree, and the costs of maintaining two homes was starting to pile up.

Dear Mom,
I'm sending you a photo of your new grandson, Walid. Aziza and Haifa are fine, and we all miss you dearly. I'm happy to inform you that I'm also doing very well in my studies, and have built a business acumen translating and helping many businessmen. I also finished construction of my house and am planning to take the family to Sana'a in the future. My plan is to convince Aziza to also join the University; there are many opportunities here for those who speak English.

I waited and waited for my mother's reaction to my stories, and her stamp of approval for my work and accomplishments. I sent several letters with no response – but gravestones do not respond. A letter from Meriam told me about the untimely passing of my mother, in a land strange to her. Meriam said that time in Hijaz was hard on her, and she was buried near her grandfather's grave in Jeddah. The words in that letter took a while to sink in but my tears were faster than my comprehension. I already felt something was not right. She had had so much to tell me after my wedding, but we felt our unspoken words could wait until her return – an unkept promise.

I was shaking and tearful. I felt lost. It was like the ground beneath my feet had disappeared, and I had been too preoccupied with my personal life and career to listen to my mother and pay enough attention to her. Damned malaria. I needed to know how she spent her final days: *Did she leave a will? Did she say anything? Mama ... MAAAAA ...* I wanted to scream.

It was only Haifa's hug that snapped me out of it. She knew something was not right and her caring instincts offered the solace I needed. "*My mom died,*" I told Haifa, feeling numb. Then the odor of diaper-change duties snapped me back to reality and I had to regain my composure. That hug helped in many ways, my dear Haifa.

I take solace that Mother somehow knows I'm alright. That we're all alright, and will be alright.

A Tie, and a Home

Life is a series of ups and downs, peaks and troughs. The more you go through and experience, the more you realize how strong you really are, and what being a man is all about. I knew one thing, though, it wasn't easy. There was no time to sit down somewhere and rest, and taking a day off was rarely an option, especially when opportunity came knocking. One of my recurrent gigs was drafting payment instructions to the banks for processing, especially at a new foreign bank office that just opened in Sana'a the year before. The manager seemed to think I had what it took to recruit more clients, and I was happy to give it a try.

I was exhilarated to tailor my first suit, at Geneve Tailoring, which was the hallmark tailor of our times. It was navy blue and made of the more expensive fabric. I worked in banking by this point, and I had to splurge as work demanded it. Strange how one's net worth increased significantly with a suit and tie. I was doing the same job, more or less, but now on behalf of an institution, in a more formal sense. It gave me fulfillment, and I felt the need to put my money into something tangible, a piece of property in Sana'a to call home.

However, unlike my studies, working at the bank was a full-time commitment, with breaks far and few between. I longed to go home, to see my wife and two children. I had to find a different job that allowed me the flexibility I needed. And I found it on the road, translating for engineers working on the Sana'a-Taiz highway under construction. I spent many days going through this road and I had come to know it by heart. But nothing was like coming home to my family every day. I had to convince Aziza to move to Sana'a.

This was hard on her too, but I remained too selfish to see it from her side, and continued to ask for what I wanted. *We must look into the future*, I kept on reiterating, *what it brings for our young family, and the unrealized dreams of the big city*. I kept on recounting stories to Aziza about the University, about the classes and interactions, and the joy that brought. I think I recruited her to follow in my footsteps. I kept pushing until she was ready to pursue her own education and become the first woman in the region to pursue a college degree.

Aziza didn't finish secondary education because there was no accessible secondary school, but she was smart and hardworking. I went to see Mr Jabir Afif regarding her enrollment. He already knew me from various University functions and could see that there were barely any women enrolled in the University, so he agreed to enroll her as an unregistered student for the first year and assess thereafter. If she kept up with the work and proved herself capable, then that year would be considered in lieu of the standard admissions requirements, and she would be registered formally from the next year onwards.

Aziza got accustomed to life in Sana'a quickly this time around. We had become acquainted with distant relatives who also made a life in the big city. Haifa and Walid were growing fast, and I finally completed my degree, and even got the honor of having a short version of my graduation thesis published in the University's first edition of its *Journal of English*, entitled "The Nature of Conflict in The Hairy Ape," reflecting on the famous work by Eugene O'Neill. I also landed a job with the government, working at the television station to produce Yemen's first English-language news program, catering to the growing expat population in Yemen in my best American English accent. The schedule worked well between Aziza's morning classes and my work in the afternoons to produce the show that I broadcast live in the evening, around 11pm.

That was until the fateful day I met the President, and Robert arranged for me to pursue higher education in the United States through a Fulbright Scholarship.

Chapter 5: America Calling

I was admitted to a Master of Arts program at Ohio State University, in Athens, Ohio. Robert called me to see him the week after our meeting at the Embassy. This was big news. Part of me felt that I didn't want to shake the boat and rather focus on my career, but the real reason was my fear of the unknown. I was starting to go through what Aziza went through when she moved to Sana'a – going to a strange place where no one knows you. Plus, it won't be the first time I let an opportunity go.

I discussed this with Aziza, and to my surprise she wanted me to go and she wanted to join me with the kids in the USA. I was taken aback with how this village girl had been transformed as a result of her university experience. The program itself had come a long way since I first enrolled, and now there are larger numbers of students, more content, and several US Peace Corp lecturers and support staff. This time of heavy indoctrination at Sana'a University had turned my sweet rural wife into a cowboy. Howdy, partner! This happened so fast.

A week later, I met with Robert – and six other young men who also got admissions under the Fulbright Program – for our pre-departure briefing. They seemed to be more confident about what would happen next. We all were spread out to different parts of the USA. They were distinguished young men, many of whom I continued to be friends with for a long time. It was June 1976, and I was due to travel in September. My plan was to get settled, then send for Aziza and the kids to join me. It was a three-year program and Aziza was most keen to experience the US first hand. She would have finished her bachelor's degree by then as well.

It was a long and arduous journey. Back in the 1970s, flying on a plane was intimidating in its own right, and we needed to fly some thirty hours to Washington, DC for an orientation week. There were hundreds of us and I met other going to my same University hailing from all sorts of places. I connected with an Iranian fellow named Kamran - the only other Muslim in our small group - hoping to find in him some comforts of home, and I suspect he the same.

Kamran was an extravert and pushed me to join him in touring Washington, DC. Kamran and I took the opportunity to roam around the city, and connect directly with Americans and fellow tourists on the streets and try to get a feel for the area. Some encounters were more pleasant than others, but the majestic buildings surrounded by greenery were most memorable, and it was wonderful to see the National Mall and just be a tourist like in the brochures. I had so much to write to Aziza about.

We made it to Athens, Ohio, a couple of days later. It was an odd feeling to think of this forest-like place as my new home for the next few years. It took me a while to shake the feeling of being a Stranger in the land of Strange. But I needed to settle-in, focus on what was important, and get on with the program. Kamran seemed to be more organized and knew what he was doing. He had had the opportunity of conversing with prior Fulbright scholarships who shared with him tips and tricks and what to do. He kept on warning me to keep an eye for racism, hippy culture, and counterculture.

People were mostly friendly, engaging, and open. I was starting to get used to the pace of life in Athens, and had a few polaroid photos taken that I sent to Aziza, including my picture in a Bobcats pullover - sent inside *Readers Digest* magazine - as per my old habit.

My dearest Aziza,
Sending you my best greetings from America, life is going well and I am pursuing the program smoothly. I've also started a part-time job with the University's newspaper that gave me an opportunity to meet many students. It is getting really cold here but I hope to bring you and the kids after the winter season.

Love,
Abdulaziz

Dear Abdulaziz,
We miss you dearly. Haifa is doing well and she is doing very well in school, Walid is also doing well. They are well behaved and very good kids. All is fine with us we just miss you a lot. Don't worry about making arrangements for us so soon, as it will probably have to wait a bit more and you'll need to buy one more ticket. I give you the great news that I'm expecting our third child, the greatest blessing we could have.

By the way, your father and Ghaya got a divorce. I knew their marriage wouldn't last long...

Love,
Aziza

My dear Aziza,
I received your message and the wonderful news. I'll be sending you some cash soon to help with the expenses. Let's make plans to arrange for you and the kids to come to America over the summer, it will be better then and Haifa will love it here. Start teaching her some English.

Love,
Abdulaziz

Dreaming Bigger

Kamran had frequented weekend trips to Columbus, Ohio, which took around two hours by bus. Almost half the bus were students - like us - who wanted to enjoy the thrill of the big city over the weekend, the big city that had so much to offer that young men like us would want. Flashy lights, loud music, good times. The plan was to sleep over at the home of an acquaintance of Kamran who attended the University at Columbus. I was game, eager to see what this brought about.

What struck me most was how lavishly these young men lived. They rented their own place outside the dormitory, many of them owned their own cars, and they spent a lot on clubs, going on dates, and all sorts of games and activities. The answer was jobs. Competitive wages were something that small towns often lacked. Perhaps I could move here instead of staying in Small Town USA and earn more. Kamran had the same thought, but he had other spending priorities.

Upon return, I went to the guidance counselor asking about transfer options. To my surprise, she informed me that I also got admission to the Master of Public Administration (MPA) at Harvard University in Boston according to her query - Thank you, Robert. Since my funding covered three years, I might be able to salvage most of it and move some credits to pursue that program. The counselor strongly encouraged me to pursue this, noting that Harvard was a most reputed University and not many people were granted admission there.

So now I had a new plan. It actually worked like a dream. Not only did some of the credits I had already earned count toward the MPA, but I could double count them toward both degrees so long as I maintained my enrollment at both Universities. Obviously, I needed to cover some additional fees but I thought I could make it work. But first, I had to survive the Ohio winter while the paperwork went through both Universities and secure Fulbright approval for my transfer.

The approval came by at late spring, just a couple of weeks after Nadia, my third child, was born. I was set to start the next semester at Harvard in the fall, and I had a lot of work to do and needed to make the necessary arrangements over the summer. But first, I asked Kamran to give me some driving lessons.

Moving to Boston

Boston had a faster tempo to it; so did Harvard. I knew I had to make this dual study arrangement work. Fulbright gave me a couple of Yemeni student contacts in Boston who could help me settle in. They had leased an apartment not too far from campus to give them some space away from the loud college lifestyle, and I was welcome to join them so long I chipped in with the rent. Living out of a suitcase and on a couch was necessary until I got on my feet, as I awaited Aziza and the kids' arrival to Boston. It took longer than I initially thought but I finally got it sorted out.

Aziza and the kids were expected on the August 19, 1977, at Logan Airport. I waited and waited. Maybe they missed their flight? Maybe they got lost? I didn't know what to think. After six hours of waiting I thought perhaps I had missed them walking out and they took a taxi and went ahead? I had given Aziza the address and phone number. So I drive back to the house; no sign of them. Back to the airport information desk; no one could help me. I thought to myself they had likely missed their flight, so I went home, but I stopped by the apartment where the guys were to pick up a few items I had left behind.

"*Abdulaziz, someone called for you a few minutes ago, some lady,*" my roommate said.

"*What? Who...?*" thinking to myself it might be from one of the jobs I applied for when I first arrived. I wondered if I should I call now or call later, but then I thought *Let me call now since they just called and the phone is right there, plus I won't have to pay for this phone call since I'm using their phone...* Calling the number, it appeared it was the information desk from Logan Airport. My family was there, but they had been rerouted on a different plane and arrived late on a domestic flight an hour ago. Ah, what a relief. Aziza had jotted down every telephone number from every place I moved to in the USA to keep track of me. She was a smart woman.

It was such a challenge and a risk to have Aziza and the kids fly across two continents and an ocean by themselves. It was Aziza's first flight experience, and with three kids, it would have been difficult. I had confidence in her, though. She spoke English and would be able to manage. In addition, money was tight and it would have been expensive to buy my own return ticket to bring them, not to mention the work days I would have had to forfeit. But at last our family was reunited.

Boston was kind to us. I finished my program at Ohio State and progressed very well at Harvard. It was such a wonderful feeling to come home to my family, to hold my kids. Watching them enjoy the greenery and experience the snow. Life was perfect, had it not been for the ticking clock until my Master's degree ended.

What struck me most was how much independent learning the programs required. Students were expected to identify the issues on their own, find solutions, and spend much time at the library researching and investigating. I must confess I enjoyed the MPA program much more than the MA in English; studying Shakespeare and *MacBeth* was one thing, but investigating public policy and finances was another. My professors were most generous with their time, and I'd come to learn a lot about how the seemingly big transactions to import wood and other materials by big Yemeni businessmen were most pitiful compared to almost everything else in this world.

In retrospect, we only learn as far as we can see. If we can see further, then we can learn more and grow. My time in Boston was profoundly different from Ohio. The work opportunities were also significantly more varied and enriching. I worked as a typist with a literary agent. My job was to retype printed pages of books while incorporating editors' remarks, suggestions, and other edits to produce a clean page. I enjoyed that work, as I became privy to the minds of authors and editors, how to say things better, more succinctly, and improve the experience of readers. The best thing about this work was the flexibility in terms of timing and choice of assignments. I would often find myself editing pre-publication best sellers on a variety of topics from politics to culture.

Having that kind of exposure also affected my personal development and academic performance at the University. My professors noticed, and they encouraged me to pursue further learning, and consider applying for a PhD. Thankfully the stars aligned. A PhD, however, was a different ballgame. I needed to reapply for another Fulbright doctoral scholarship that might or might not materialize. I also needed to identify what it is that I wanted to research.

My first inclination was on how to achieve prosperity. How to transform the Yemeni economy to resemble something closer to a more developed one. In my pursuit of developing a thesis statement and seeking guidance from supervisors, I was invited to attend some lectures in international economics. I was intrigued by this area of work and decided that I might as well sign up for these classes. Having just concluded the requirements for the MA in English at Ohio State, I had time to pursue a third degree. Why not, especially since it would open the door to a PhD.

My Fulbright PhD approval came through in early 1979, two years into my Master's degree. I joined the PhD program at Tufts University, not too far from Harvard University campus. My PhD research was titled "The structural transformation of the Yemeni economy" and it promised a recipe for Yemen's prosperity. At the same time, I found myself gravitating to Tufts' Master's Program in Law and Diplomacy, in addition to pursuing the PhD. I was taking advantage of my time there to the fullest and would pursue all I could, for as long I could.

I must admit that the intellectual life and engagement in the academic community was most fulfilling. Perhaps I could contribute to this life at the University that put me on this path, at Sana'a University. Aziza was of the same view as well. She had just started a Hubert H. Humphrey fellowship, and was keen on building educational systems to help people fulfill their full potential. It was our turn to contribute to our society, and education was the best path to pursue.

Easier said than done. I still had some way to go until my program ran its course through 1983. I had applied to join the faculty at Sana'a University and start a new career as an educator at the College of Economy and Commerce, and I felt my chances were favorable.

Chapter 6: And Back to Yemen

In July 1982, Aziza and I were blessed with our fourth child, Raidan. He's the last of the gang. I was also appointed as a professor of Economics at Sana'a University just before that, and that appointment also included a subsidized apartment at the faculty residency and a generous benefits package by Yemen's standards, thanks to Kuwaiti funding. The best part was the academic community feeling, where our neighbors were also mainly young families in similar situations, building a wonderful sense of comradery and a focus on our mission in uplifting our nation through education.

The kids seemed to be prospering too. Having spent the last five years in the USA, their Arabic language skills had suffered, so I was keen that they retain their English while building up their Arabic. School was next door and the University campus was in close proximity too. I loved sitting on the floor around a plate of fava beans with the family around me, asking about classes and stories about the neighbors. My trusty Volvo station wagon, bought off an outgoing diplomat, hauled our family of six wherever we needed to go.

Abdulaziz, You're a Machine

My focus was creating academic content that was both rich and relevant. The Faculty of Commerce had relied on recycled materials, some from Egyptian universities, others commissioned, bought, or borrowed. I had been given two subjects to teach for first year students, namely an Introduction to Economics and the Principles of Finance. I was a junior lecturer and didn't have much teaching experience – plus I'd be delivering this content in Arabic despite my education in English – so I worked under the mentorship of more established colleagues.

The first order of business was to flesh out the curricula to the key concepts students needed to learn. I wanted to bring the education practices I learnt in the USA to Sana'a University, and consulted heavily with my colleagues and peers who were in similar situations. Our collective goal was to offer the best quality education we could. So I thought it would be simplest if I just authored some books to serve as one-stop curricula to cover the subjects I taught. Tens of books had already passed through my hands and I was used to this.

My first book, *Theories in Public Finances in the Arab Republic of Yemen* was well received. Too well, I might add. It was encouraging to see students able to refer to the content, and the administration even sent copies to be deposited at universities across the region as a sign that Sana'a University had "arrived" and was able to produce quality content. It was also to encourage fellow faculty members to do the same.

By 1984, I had produced three more publications in addition to the first book; a two-part book series entitled *Simplified Economics*, and a chapter in an English-language book on Yemen's public finances that resonated with my first book. This work got me promoted to becoming the head of the Economics section at the faculty, a welcome bump in pay and prestige. I was asked to keep publishing and expand my work to various topics relevant to policymakers' priorities at the time. I have authored and coauthored journal articles and studies on local finance, energy production and consumption, urbanization, public investment, public service, among other topics. It has become second nature to me to be productive. I was used to going through one manuscript after the other during my time in the USA, and with my trusty typewriter I could go on and on like a musician with his instrument. I had a reputation at the faculty of being "a machine," as I seemed to churn out publications seemingly effortlessly. But no, it was indeed a lot of effort.

I also organized one of our first field research undertakings to assess public finances during that time. I had a few of my students visit the Deputy Governor of the central bank, Dr Yahya, who was also a fellow professor at the University at the time. The goal behind that visit is to connect theory to practice and to understand more about the real-world aspects of public accounting and monetary policy. Other students went to visit the Ministry of Finance, the tax authority, and other key national institutions of relevance and come back to class to share their reflections. The task was to take a closer glimpse at the practical challenges facing the country and how theory linked to practice, but also to interview officials working in the space to develop their understanding of what it took to work in these various sectors.

For me, time was a gift - you could spend it productively, or you could spend it unproductively. Productive time yielded results, and unproductive time was a lost opportunity. I had also taken teaching roles at the National Civil Service Institute, at the Police Academy, and at other institutions of higher learning where opportunities presented themselves. If I was going to contribute to uplifting the state of higher education, then these were opportunities to do so. Needless to say, every additional work opportunity carried its own reward, both financially and for my career. I was promoted from Assistant Professor to Associate Professor by 1986, four and a half years following my initial appointment.

But then and out of nowhere, I got demoted from my role as head of the Economics Section. It came as a surprise, especially as I thought I was doing very well. My colleague who replaced me in this role broke the news to me, asking when he could take over the head's office. Apparently my "hobby" had upset the University's leadership and I had become a marked man. Tough years ahead.

Chapter 7: My "Human Rights" Hobby

In the USA, the concept of academic freedom is enshrined in the open space for thought, dialogue, and critical challenges of established principles and anything dubbed as common knowledge. I already had developed my own insights into the human psyche while undergoing my bachelor's degree in English literature, and it was interesting to see how one person related to others and to society. It spoke to how our identities were shaped by the space we had to express ourselves, forming our views of what is right, and using our power to act upon them for the betterment of ourselves and society at large.

Plus, being born on the 24th of October was a sign, too. That was the day when the UN Charter came into force, and I felt both I and the UN Charter had a common mission to advance human rights. As a Fulbright scholar and having had the opportunity to connect with academics from across the region and the world, I felt there was something that we might be able to do collectively to elevate the stature of human rights in Yemen and in the region. In 1983, I cofounded the Arab Organization for Human Rights based in Cairo. In 1984, I was elected to serve on the board of the Amman-based Arab Thought Forum.

Apparently, establishing the Yemeni Organization for Human Rights in 1986 triggered the authorities. The security apparatus had flagged me as a "potential troublemaker" and asked the University to investigate my activities. The key concern was that giving me a platform to work with students, and promoting me to head a section, could be seen as an endorsement of my actions. I must say, I expected some pushback for the organization, but I hadn't expected it to be this swift or harsh. One day, I was called in to see the dean, to find him seated next to two gentlemen; one looked familiar but the other didn't.

"*Dr Abdulaziz Al-Saqqaf, welcome. Come sit,*" said the dean, adding, "*We took the decision to temporarily hold your post as head of the Economics section due to your recent political activity.*"

"*What political activity?*" I asked.

"*You applied to establish the Yemeni Organization for Human Rights, along with a few persons who are under investigation due to their engagement in the violence taking place in South Yemen,*" he added.

I had prepared responses to defend my decision to establish the organization, citing Article 25 of the constitution that guarantees the right for expression and even the political guidance from the General People Congress (GPC) as the ruling party that had language to advance freedoms. But I must confess that I did not see the security angle based on the violence taking place in South Yemen as a reason to curtail this work.

"*We, as educators, have a responsibility toward our citizens and country. We want to open avenues for civilized dialogue to facilitate cooperation and help us better our country,*" I responded.

At which point the unfamiliar gentleman interrupted, "*Then call it organization for dialogue, for cooperation, not for human rights. It is bad enough that you're sending your students to snoop around all over the place.*"

I felt conflicted at that moment. Some of my students had reported strange things going on with public finances, and we all knew there was some corruption and irregularities were expected. However, that gentleman looked like he spoke out of order and revealed too much information, judging by the reaction of the dean.

"We will not stop you from doing this human rights work, but it must be done outside the university and not involve the students. And I would encourage you to wait until the political situation in the South cools down before taking any further steps," the dean concluded.

This would not be easy. It was a slap on the hand, so to speak. It could have been worse, but I suspected that my work and reputation shielded me from sharper, and potentially more severe, reactions. I also wondered what I was going to tell Aziza. The problem in being a tight-knit community like the teaching staff was that word spread easily. Not only was my successor as the head of the department a neighbor in our residential complex, but there was also as gossip around this meeting that would spread like wildfire.

Things like this are demoralizing, but little did I know that this would be the norm over the next many years. I needed to reach through to people about how human rights weren't something to be worried about, rather were a great enabler for peace, prosperity, and a better tomorrow for all, especially those on the fringes of society. And it was upon us, as the educated elite, to advance them.

But I swallowed my pride, kept my head down, and continued to churn out materials. I authored a few more academic papers and journal articles, including two new books on Islamic Economic Principles and on Islamic Banking. Those books were also special to me as I moved on from my typewriter to my first IBM personal computer. Not only was it easier to produce and edit, but also made formatting easier and was more forgiving of errors.

Following a year-long hiatus from engaging in human rights activities, I decided it was time to revive this conversation. In 1988, I published a book under the title *Human Rights*, on the occasion of the 50th anniversary of the Universal Declaration of Human Rights. I knew I was taking a risk, but I felt strongly about publishing this book to popularize the concept of human rights, raise awareness of Yemen's own commitments under local and international conventions, and have a collective conversation on our aspirations as Yemenis. This book was designed to be an authority in Arabic about what human rights were, how to understand them within the context of Sharia law and current legislation, and how to apply them. It was nonconfrontational in the sense that it only clarified what already existed, but it was designed to educate and raise awareness.

And yes, there was a backlash, though silent this time. Simply put, I was relieved of all my teaching duties at the University, where lecturers were assigned subjects and classes to teach and I was given none, and hours teaching classes had been a good two-thirds of my pay. It was a power move to get me to petition to get classes, but the real question for me concerned the price tag on my willingness to stop pushing for the ideals of human rights.

My book, *Human Rights*, published in early 1988, created a big stir beyond Yemen's borders, too. Invitations to participate in regional and international conferences and engagements flocked my way. Having no commitment to classes, I participated in several of these conferences. I also spent two months in Japan as a part of a fellowship with Japan's Institute of Developing Economies, where I published a book entitled *Meiji Japan's Experience as Model for Third World Development*, followed by several months in Washington, DC working at the World Bank's headquarters under the Robert McNamara fellowship program. That was both an opportunity to work with the world's best, as well as a chance to network. A lot that happens in Washington, DC influences the wider world, and having the opportunity to take a glimpse into that wider world was more than eye-opening.

The fellowship provided first-hand experience to work on World Bank projects of relevance, and through my academic work I realized that access to finance was the choke point that limited Yemen's development. We needed serious money to build the infrastructure that could propel us into the modern world. That money was accessible, it just required some legwork to get it to flow. During my time in the USA, I also connected with several academic groups working on the region, including Georgetown's Center for Arab Studies, and I did a short stint as a visiting scholar at the University of Texas at Austin. However, I cut that stint short following a job offer that came through to head the Arab Institute for Banking Studies, based in Amman, Jordan.

My sabbatical with Sana'a University was extended, and I felt our dean breathe a sigh of relief when I asked for an extended leave to take on the job in Amman in 1989. Perhaps being physically out of the country would help calm down the stir I had been making, and getting me preoccupied with professional engagements as opposed to giving me more time for my human rights hobby.

But I'm no hobbyist. My two-year contract with the Institute ended prematurely. This was my second lesson in how geopolitics, seemingly afar, was actually much closer to home.

Saleh & Saddam: Best Buddies

In July 1978, Ali Abdullah Saleh came to power in Northern Yemen as the fourth president in a span of two years. Turbulent times marked Saleh's ascent into power, starting with a purge of rivals, but he moved quickly to stabilize the country and wrestle power away from any potential rivals or threats. The story goes that President Saleh's first international engagement following his ascent was in November 1978, where he traveled to Baghdad to attend the Arab Summit. Upon his arrival, he was received by Iraq's Saddam Hussein in the customary welcome meeting, however Saddam wasn't impressed by Saleh's look. At this point, Saddam took Saleh aside at the Presidential Palace, walked him to his private quarters, and called on the presidential barber to get a haircut, and the presidential tailor to get him a well-fitted suit. An hour later, Saddam flattered Saleh saying, "*Now you look Presidential.*"

The two leaders hit it off quickly after that, with Saddam sending advisors, offering training opportunities, and coordinating positions on all relevant matters to both countries and leaders. Saleh always made sure he had a proper haircut before meeting Saddam, but he was also keen on replicating Iraq's success in nation-building, military-building, and intelligence development, having himself spent some time in Iraq previously. Relations between the two countries grew much closer during the pursuant decade, culminating in Yemen joining the Arab Cooperation Council with Iraq, along with Jordan and Egypt.

In addition to the odd battalion to participate in the Iraq-Iran war, thousands of Yemeni students were fielded to Iraq over the 1980s, including many of our students at the University. Yemen proved to be a fertile ground to Baathist ideas brought back from Iraq, including anti-Iranian sentiments accompanying the Iraq-Iran war, and the broader rhetoric for pan-Arabism. Having multiple political schools of thoughts laid the first seeds for political pluralism in the country, especially after the Nasserites' purge in the late 1970s. I myself authored two journal articles on inter-Arab trade and investment and barriers to Arab economic integration during this time.

However, as the cold war started to fade out in the late 1980s, the West's interests in Yemen also started to dwindle. This left a space for significant open rapprochement between the Saleh and Saddam regimes, subsequently allowing the rise of Baathist propaganda and tolerating recruitment that was undertaken in the open. The zeal of pan-Arabism reached unprecedented levels and contributed significantly to accelerating unification between North and South Yemen. A key example was how similarities increased between left-leaning Baathist messaging in the North and Socialist/Marxist messaging in the South, accelerated further by the collapse of the Soviet Union. This was the opposite effect of what the USA and the West were trying to do in Yemen just a decade before.

Both North and South needed a fresh start, and Yemen adopted a strange mélange of military-empowered pluralistic proletariat rule with both Islamic and socialist leanings. This could be a promising democracy or a disaster in the making, or both together. And I was missing in action while this was going on, first in Washington, DC, then in Amman.

With Iraqi influence, all members of the Arab Cooperation Council took less-than-honorable positions in relation to the Iraqi invasion of Kuwait, but none of them were as vulnerable as Yemen. On November 29, 1990, Yemen, which occupied a UN Security Council Seat at the time, voted against Security Council Resolution 678 authorizing military action to force Iraq out of Kuwait. In response, Yemen lost the little Western aid it received and the significant support it had derived from its neighbors, principally through expelling close to a million Yemeni expatriate workers who provided close to two-thirds of foreign exchange through remittances. It was a disaster on all counts.

Jordan and Egypt were also in hot water, given their relationship with Saddam. And my work contract was one of the casualties when Saddam threatened to spread the war across the region. And honestly, I needed to get back to Yemen where the action was. We were on a plane back to Sana'a in October 1990, a few months after Yemeni unification and just before the first Gulf War.

The mood back In Sana'a was profoundly different. On the one hand, this new air of multiparty pluralism and open space for media and civil liberties brought by unification was most promising. On the other hand, it was also quite daunting as this was unchartered territory for all of us. Two authoritarian regimes with no democratic experience whatsoever had come together to create a democracy, are now they were both openly tolerating dissent and different opinions. We've never been in a situation like this before, with open and public confrontations at the highest levels, particularly in the face of the socioeconomic turmoil associated with the dual frustrations of having to cater to a million newly deported citizens and losing the significant remittance income they used to send.

This was a challenging, unprecedented, and most fragile situation. We needed help. Yemen needed help. We needed the help of our neighbors, of our friends, and of the world to successfully maneuver through this challenging time. I had a responsibility to my students, myself, and my country folk to contribute to addressing this situation.

Making Yemen a Good World Citizen

Upon my return to Sana'a University I was reinstated as an active full professor. Thereafter, I consulted with colleagues and peers on their takeaways about the country's transformation and all the accelerating developments. I particularly reached out to the professors working on the newly established Political Sciences program, fishing for ideas on what this transition meant and how we could contribute. Excitement was in the air, despite this untested political arrangement. Previous concerns on academic freedoms had dwindled and we were all looking forward to realizing our collective aspirations as a people united.

The problem was that democracy wasn't our collective preference; it was the only way the two political parties that controlled the North and the South parts of Yemen respectively could coexist in one country. This meant a multiparty system became a necessity, and teaching two ruling parties to compete or share power was going to be a lot of work. Needless to say, the first year of a multiparty system resulted in a mushrooming of political parties and other groupings.

Someone needed to keep an eye on this Yemeni great democracy experiment and find a way to get the world invested in its success. That could be my role, through *Yemen Times*, Yemen's first English-language newspaper.

Why an English-language newspaper you ask? Two reasons. First because English is the language of the world, and it is the language of our present civilization. If it is not your first language, it should be your second. A newspaper because Yemen had a problem communicating with the world, and having an independent newspaper would make it both a credible and truthful actor in sending that message across to all concerned parties.

I finally spent several weeks with *The Star*, a weekly newspaper coming out of Amman. I consulted with Osama Sherif, the editor and publisher of the paper, to see how it worked, and engaged him in a contract to do proper systems, information, and technology transfer. Thus *Yemen Times* was born, starting with two small SE Classic Macintosh machines.

It was a most humble beginning. The total *Yemen Times* team was three people – a typist/page setter, a messenger/assistant, and me. We did all the financial and administrative work. We did everything from interviews, to newswriting, to pagination and supervising printing of the paper, to distribution. But we made it work, and the first *Yemen Times* issue was on its way.

Part Two: Yemen Times

Chapter 8: Introducing Yemen Times

In my first editorial, I introduced *Yemen Times* as an *independent weekly paper not attached to any political party of thought.* It would cover mainly two categories of activities, Economic/Business news, as well as Democracy and Human Rights. I felt these were the two pillars of my work and life, making *Yemen Times* the conduit of my vision for Yemen's transition, betterment, and to the country's own contributions to the world under the Motto: Making Yemen a Good World Citizen.

What would make Yemen become a good world citizen, you ask? It was the adoption of democratic values and observation of human rights. Yemen must chart its own course based on a critical merit-based evaluation of its options. The last couple of years were particularly taxing on Yemen's wellbeing following the Iraqi invasion of Kuwait, but the country was still pulling through, and hopefully, with democratic dialogue, we would be able to course-correct the mistakes of the past.

I knew that the first edition of *Yemen Times* would cause a stir, being the first and only English-language newspaper in the country. I'd learnt a few lessons along the way, in terms of how useful the expatriate community in Yemen found the English-language local news broadcast in the 1970s. This community had expanded and now included diplomats, businessmen, elite, and other influential persons who literally connected Yemen with the world. *Yemen Times* would be a key medium to connect with that audience, in my own terms, and engage them to constructively contribute toward making Yemen a good world citizen.

I also needed to have President Saleh's picture grace the cover of the first *Yemen Times* edition. Given the fluid political situation and the transition, I had to go out of my way to show that this was a constructive tool to help Yemen – from an independent point of view – through sending Yemeni voices to the world. I picked a picture of President Saleh with a head full of hair resembling his pre-Saddam hairstyle, meaning to say, *Mr President, be yourself, be proud, and don't let others push you around.* That picture was attached to a news story about his interview with a leftist-leaning Egyptian newspaper explaining Yemen's position vis-a-vis the Gulf War.

Establishing a newspaper is hard work, demanding a lot of financial, human, and political capital. I used my savings to buy the two computers and other machines, learned layout and typesetting, and marshaled all my experience in journalism, editing, and publishing. I also opted to publish it every Wednesday ahead of Yemen's Thursday–Friday weekend, taking a page from my Ohio experience where the student newspaper was published just before the weekend so that folks will have something to read during their free time.

Yemen Times got license number 9 for the year 1991, from Yemen's Ministry of Information: the other eight were either official newspapers or political-party led. I was happy with that number, noting that the mushrooming of political parties and groupings also translated into a wide spectrum of newspapers and magazines, reaching eighty-eight by April 1991, voicing all sorts of opinions, agendas, and often polarizing perspectives.

YEMEN  TIMES

YEMEN'S ONLY ENGLISH-LANGUAGE WEEKLY

SANA'A, 27 FEBRUARY - 5 MARCH, 1991, VOL 1, NUMBER 1

INSIDE

Dr. Iryani: YEMEN has Taken an Independent Position regardless of the external pressure p.3

Yemenis are outraged by aggression against Iraq p. 12

- The Budget for 1991 Approved. *pages 6+7*
- The Constitution of Yemen *page 5*
- Discovery of an 8000 Year Temple *page 10*
  *****

OUR*VIEWPOINT*

Introducing the YEMEN TIMES

THIS IS The first issue of the Yemen Times. Therefore, it is with pleasure that I use this editorial to introduce it to the reader.

The YEMEN TIMES is an independent weekly paper not attached to any political party or thought. As such, its stand vis-avis the various local, regional, and international issues is determined on the basis of an objective assessment of the merits and demerits involved. The paper aims to reach out to a large base of readers, specially amongst the intellectual classes, the decision makers, the business sector, and the international community.

Nevertheless, the paper covers with interest and commitment two categories of activities, which are:

1. Economic/Business Activities:

YEMEN TIMES will provide a detailed coverage of economic and business activities in Yemen, and a synopsis of important regional and international issues in this sector. Major emphasis will be placed on trade, investments, economic laws, tenders, and market-watch aspects in price levels, consumption, interest rates, exchange rates, etc. In general, government and private-sector efforts in the country's socio-economic development process will be extensively covered.

2. Democracy and Human Rights:

YEMEN TIMES believes that the prosperity and strength of nations, if at least in the long run, will depend on democratic values and the observation of human rights. In the absence of these two basic elements in society, it is doubtful that much can be achieved. Therefore, the paper will closely follow those two issues as reflected in Yemeni life. Much has been achieved in both counts in the recent past, and much more remains to be achieved.

The paper will heavily depend on primary sources of information; i.e., interviews, polls, field surveys, and contributions and feed-back from our readers. Yet the paper will also provide information from secondary sources, specially through the weekly summary round-up of the local press. All in all, YEMEN TIMES hopes to be informative and analytic in nature. All members of the paper promise to make a sincere effort to serve our readership, and all of us will appreciate an active participation and feed-back. Till next Wednesday, take care!

PRESIDENT SALEH: YEMEN IS UNITED IN ITS STAND!

President Ali Abdullah Saleh confirmed that Yemen and the Arab Nation will strive for an independent Arab resolution for the Gulf crisis. He reaffirmed opposition to the imperialist-zionist offensive which aims to keep the Arab homeland under its custody. President Saleh made this statement during an interview with the Egyptian weekly "Alyasar" magazine.

"The Arab nation will never forsake its independence whatever the situation," the Yemeni President was quoted as saying. We believe that the Arab people stand firmly with Iraq in its historic struggle against the Western onslaught, he said. Referring to the economic block of Iraq, the Yemeni President said it was invalid that it is a ploy to exert pressure on Iraq.

Within Yemen, the President said that the crisis creased cohesion among Yemenis and deepened unity. "Despite the negative economic impact, the smear campaign orchestrated againt the country, we in Yemen stand steadfast to our position. We will not be drawn in the media thrashing, said. Commenting on last Arab summit held Cairo, President Ali Abdullah Saleh said that he not wish to see the Arab summit fail follow the return of the Arab League headquarters Cairo. With regard to Yemeni-Egyptian relation he confirmed those relations were deeply rooted and strong enough to withstand any events. pointed to the effective Egyptian contribution the September and October revolutions in Yemen. "one can change or affect the solid relations between the two peoples, not even differences among the rulers and regimes," said.

Finally, he said Yemen's consitution based on Islamic values which it cannot violate.

PRICE PER COPY IN YEMEN 10 Y.R.
ANNUAL SUBSCRIPTIONS (INCLUDES POSTAGE/DELIVERY AND HANDLING): YEMEN; US$80, MIDDLE EAST US$ 150, ELSEWHERE US$ 250

Reception to *Yemen Times* was positive. I had printed just under a thousand copies and drove myself across newsstands and bookstores asking them to put it on display and sell at a 20% margin. I also made sure that I had enough copies to distribute to friends and potential allies, such as senior officials with whom I wanted to engage in subsequent editions. It was a lot of work, and our small team was able to see it through. Luckily my aggressive promotion for the newspaper would soon yield return through advertising revenue to help rescue my dwindling savings.

I also received a call from the Ministry of Information, saying that my coverage was appreciated and that I should do more to explain Yemen's position to the world, away from misconceptions. The second edition of *Yemen Times* included exactly that, an analysis by yours truly that explained the Yemeni perspective: *"Yemen's position has been misunderstood intentionally and unintentionally. As early as August 3rd [1990], President Saleh told visiting Iraqi First Deputy Prime Minister Taha Yaseen Ramadhan that Iraq must withdraw from Kuwait.* Adding that *Yemen is treated as if it condoned the Iraqi occupation of Kuwait when it didn't."* Yemen's view was to seek a peaceful and a regional solution to have Iraq withdraw from Kuwait, and to avoid destroying Iraq as a punishment it for its invasion of Kuwait.

As a young democracy, it was in Yemen's best interest to go as far as it possibly could to build bridges with the world, and I was happy to play my part in that and engage constructively. Plus it was be useful to carry favors, as I was sure I would be needing to call on those favors soon. I was in prison in less than a month after the first edition of *Yemen Times* was published, but as a journalist examining the conditions and publishing some understanding of what it was like, I knew the risks that my line of work might bring.

The dual hat of professor-turned-journalist gave me an air of creditworthiness and receptiveness. Journalism is serious business, and I had every intention of maintaining the independence of *Yemen Times* and keeping it partial only to human rights and whatever would contribute to making Yemen a good world citizen. I also started making the rounds within the diplomatic community, international organizations, and all policymakers who would meet with me to introduce *Yemen Times*, solicit views, and show them a level of professionalism in journalism that would make them testify to *Yemen Times*'s value added in Yemen's media scene.

A useful feature in *Yemen Times* was the weekly review of the Yemeni Press, where a summary of key headlines, editorials, and highlights of partisan Arabic-language newspapers were presented for *Yemen Times*'s audiences. The idea was to help them improve their understanding on what issues were pressing to which parties, and the various perspectives emerging in Yemen's up and coming democracy. I even started getting calls from some of these newspapers flagging their upcoming headlines for inclusion in this weekly review, so that the diplomats would know where they stood.

Chapter 9: Tribulations of a Young Democracy

It was smooth sailing, until it wasn't. Yemen's fledgling democracy was starting to ache. The one-year anniversary of the country's Unification was both a milestone to celebrate as well as a moment for reflection, where contrasting ideologies had been battling it out in political life. Islamists didn't look too kindly at left-leaning socialists and took issue with other Islamists across the theological spectrum, while Baathists and Nasserists had their own power struggles. These struggles rippled all over Yemen, further exacerbating socioeconomic tensions that different strands of society faced, particularly the recent deportees from the Gulf countries. These deportees felt that they were paying the price for

---

6 ISSUES   YEMEN TIMES   **24 APRIL 1991**

POLITICAL AWARENESS AMONG YEMENI PRIMARY SCHOOL CHILDREN

YEMEN TIMES sponsored a field survey of the degree of politicization of Yemeni children. A random selection of three primary schools (Azal Modern School, Haddah, and Martyr Dailamy School) were visited by the YEMEN TIMES team. Children of ages seven to ten years (grades second, third, and fourth) were chosen as the the sample base. The children were asked several questions, and the number of children who volunteered answers were guaged, and the various answers were checked.

The major conclusions that YEMEN TIMES draws from the results are:
1) Yemeni children are far more politicized than we think.
2) The media has become an important factor in shaping the impressions of our children.
3) The recent Gulf Crisis has left a definite mark on the feelings and perceptions of our children.
There are many implications to the results of our limited survey. First and foremost, the society must determine exactly what it is it wants the children to

It is important at this stage, for the educational, cultural, and media experts and officials to draw up an appropriate policy for reporting local, regional and international issues. It will be very hard to re-educate our children once they are older, specially if they are fed inappropriate ideas today. Maybe Sanaa and Aden Universities as well as other institutions can carry out surveys to evaluate the degree to which our children are influenced by the media.

erratic decision-making in Yemen that had cost them their livelihoods and futures, and it took them a while to slowly adjust to their new lives in Yemen.

But the light shines brightest at the darkest hour. Following a year of turbulence, hardship and uncertainty, the unified Parliament, comprising of the joint legislatures of North and South, summoned the cabinet for a hearing and questioned it on a wide variety of issues, ranging from security to the economy. This sort of event was unprecedented in the history of Yemen or the region, where – for a brief moment, Yemen resembled a mature democracy with a civilized and frank discussion, ongoing publicly on key critical governance issues. The parliamentary representatives did their job very well and proved that they were not bored with details and that they knew the technical aspects of the topics under discussion. "*We share your concerns on most of these issues, and we ask for your cooperation in tackling them*," said Prime Minister Hayder Abu-Baker Al-Attas in mid-May 1991.

Furthermore, the Presidential council led by President Saleh failed twice in extracting parliamentary approval for the National Defense Council's law, and at one point it looked like the usual lobbying and under-the-table deals had proved futile, escalating the showdown between the executive and legislative branches due to frictions among the political elite in both bodies. In parallel, four newspapers and the Ministry of Information went to court, accusing each other of not having much respect for either the law or due process. A closer look at this shows there was no love lost between the two sides, noting that the Minister of Information himself and the four newspapers involved all hailed from Aden in South Yemen.

This charged political atmosphere tested our collective respect for the law. Challenging a political position should be done within the boundaries of the law and with respect for the parties involved. However, when the law is underdeveloped – which was the case in our infant democracy – we find a significant gray area that tends to be abused, especially by those who were literally "the law," namely, full time officials, part-time thugs.

Then I met Mr Law.

One of the stories we published in *Yemen Times* was how the governor of Shabwa levied all sorts of financial demands on businesses that worked within the burgeoning oil sector. Obviously, these were illegitimate demands intended to pad the governor's pockets, and he acted decisively against oil sector contractors who didn't comply. Naturally, this was a story *Yemen Times* picked up, and we interviewed one of the claimants who had his installations dismantled by the governor's order, rendering his company unable to fulfill its service contract to the oil companies, affecting both production and national revenue.

I arrived at our humble office at the outskirts of Sana'a to find an SUV and a pick-up truck parked outside with armed men standing by them. Despite being armed they looked friendly, and I thought perhaps some tribal leader wanted to meet or there was a developing story. So, as I approached the door, and I asked who they were and what they wanted with a friendly but firm tone.

"*Firstly, wouldn't you invite us inside your office? It isn't appropriate for us to stay in the street,*" said the only middle-aged person in the group, who I suspected was the person in charge.

"*Of course, you all are welcome, but your weapons are not welcome. We have a no-guns policy in the office,*" I replied with a degree of confidence.

"*Al-Qabilee* [the tribesman] *doesn't move without his weapon,*" replied a second person, who was younger and seemingly fidgety.

All the others were young men, and young men at that age can be erratic sometimes.

"*You are tribesmen and you have come to the city. We are city folk and our custom here is not to walk armed into people's offices,*" I replied gazing at the group's leader.

He was quick to hand over his automatic machine gun to a third person and replied, "*We are your guests, ya Doctor Abdulaziz, and we will follow your custom.*"

This could have escalated badly, but we were not out of the woods yet. Their claim was that they wanted to know why I published "bad things" about the governor, a claim that I categorically refuted, asking him to prove it. I gave him multiple copies of *Yemen Times* asking him to show me where I published that. I had expected that he wasn't English literate and won't be able to pick it out.

Then I replied, "*What we published is what Hajj Al-Wetari* [the subcontractor] *told the President about the dispute in Ataq* [Shabwa's capital]. *And it's a good thing that you're here, I was looking for someone from the governor's office to bring in your side. Here, come, let's do an interview.*"

The show of intimidation quickly wore off, with him asking me not to publish anything more about this story. I told him I couldn't promise that since it was our job as journalists to cover newsworthy stories. Then I gave him my business card and asked for his number to contact him should anything come up, so that next time they could contribute to the story with their own perspectives.

There were two of us in the office at the time, and we thought that this sort of incident was likely to happen again in the future, and we might want to plan some contingencies on how to manage it. It was actually lucky that the governor sent his son to see me, and not just some hothead subordinate with a point to prove.

The first thing we needed to do was move from our office at the edge of town to somewhere central downtown with better access controls, preferably close to a police or high security location. We found a perfect flat adjunct to the Central Bank that fit our needs.

GPC Recruitment Attempts

I was making a splash, interviewing Ministers, diplomats, parliamentarians, senior officials, businessmen, and all sorts of opinion leaders. In this time of political turmoil, there was a lot of alliance creation, us-and-them rhetoric, and often escalating tensions. I was approached by a fellow professor at Sana'a University inviting me to join the General People's Congress (GPC), President Saleh's party. He told me that joining the party would get me some funding for the newspaper and I could be appointed in a senior government position, an easy way to get ahead.

"The answer is quite simple. It's not because I cannot find a party whose political views and philosophies I share and possibly internalize, but it is because none of the political parties show a sufficient level of democratic values in their own internal structures and decisions," I informed my colleague with a sincere tone.

"So Saqqaf," my colleague responded, *"you create your political party the way you liked, and we'll all join you."*

"Yemen Times is my political party," I replied with a smirk. *"You can join by buying a subscription. Shall I send you a subscription form?"* I further pushed: *"You can help me by subscribing for ten copies."*

The problem with our political parties is that they carried over their pre-democratic traditions into the democracy era. They were centered around the leadership figure, who was a know-it-all person, and whatever he and the circle around him decided was unanimously adopted. Similarly, the guys the boss liked were promoted and quickly rose through the ranks, and their initiatives and interests become representative of the party, and so on. But I must say that the GPC was also home to some of the most admirable Yemenis I had ever met. However, the governor of Shabwa we discussed earlier was an opportunistic senior Baathist-turned-GPC figure, and that isn't exactly a club I would want to seek membership in or wanted to represent.

My colleague was the latest attempt to invite me to join the GPC, as they needed a way to secure my loyalty to their messaging. I had no issues with the GPC and I do not want any trouble with them. I had asked to interview President Saleh but never received a reply. I had followed up again after interviewing His Majesty King Hussein of Jordan and yet again, no reply. Then I was told I could only interview President Saleh after I joined the GPC, and he would give me a series of exclusives for the newspaper. The hassle slowed down after I inked an editorial with my reasons and my intention not to join any political party in the foreseeable future.

But I was still giving the GPC trouble, as *Yemen Times* remained the sole English-language newspaper and the chief source of information for the expatriate and diplomatic community. One way they addressed *Yemen Times*'s monopoly over that audience was through a Daily English News bulletin issued by the National News Agency, Saba. The bulletin wasn't much competition for *Yemen Times*, as it merely reported on the government's news for the day in a relatively superficial manner. But it helped to comfort Yemen's political leadership that there was something in English that the government published, and something that wasn't *Yemen Times*.

Then I introduced the French Pages. Two pages with key highlights from the Yemeni scene with a bit of francophone flair. I knew that every edition of *Yemen Times* was translated at least twice, once by the National Security bureau – folks whom I'd had a brush with not too long ago at the University – and a second time at the Ministry of Information and reported in summary to the Presidential palace. So it made sense to give them more work through the French Pages, especially now that *Yemen Times* made the bump from twelve to sixteen pages at its six-month anniversary.

| 10 THE FRENCH PAGES | | 23 OCTOBER 1991 |

Une Première

Les premières pages en français du Yémen Times, le "Temps du Yémen" illustrent les progrès accomplis dans les relations entre la France et le Yémen. Dans le domaine politique, la visite du ministre d'Etat pour les Affaires Etrangères témoigne de l'accord des deux gouvernements sur les grands problèmes de la ré- aux initiatives des hommes d'affaires yéménites et français. L'excellente coopération entre P.T.C. et C.I.T. Alcatel a permis au pays de disposer du réseau téléphonique le plus performant de la région et de former un groupe de techniciens qualifiés. Mais les relations ne se limitent pas à la politique et à

LA SEMAINE

POLITIQUE INTERIEURE

Le Conseil des ministres a tenu le 23 octobre sa réunion hebdomadaire présidée par le Premier ministre Haidar Abou Bakr al-Attas. Le Conseil a approuvé l'accord de coproduction tionale sur la politique démographique. Cet événement reflète l'attachement croissant qu'accorde le Yémen à cette question. Un document en 17 points approuvé par le Conseil des ministres en septembre dernier sera au centre des débats.
- Quantitativement, il im-

Chapter 10: Turbulence begets ... Optimism?

Political turbulence affected all walks of life in Yemen, from security to vaccination campaigns, coupled with a strong air of force-fed patriotism to the nation we were yet to build or understand. My youngest son, Raidan, wrote a short essay as a school assignment on the meaning of the flag, where he used the words *Jihad* and *backwardness* in the same essay. I probed him further to see what these really mean to him, only to realize that he had also lumped in the propaganda campaigns of ... everybody, the right-wing Islamists calling for Jihad and the left-wing socialists decrying backwardness. This is a heartwarming manifestation that there was space for everybody in this newborn country.

A curious political party was the Reform Party, or Islah. Most of its membership came from the GPC ranks with an Islamist flair, and they often continued to rub shoulders in political, economic, and social life. It's head, Sheikh Al-Ahmar, had famously repeated that GPC and Islah were the same thing. It would be interesting to follow the political trajectory of this political party, and what role it could occupy, competing with the two political parties that ruled North and South Yemen, respectively.

This week's special letter:

Raydan A. Al-Saqqaf, is a nine-year old boy in the fourth grade. He sent to us the following letter:

From Revolution to Unity: Yemeni unity was achieved on 22nd May, 1990, after the country was split by British colonial rule. Yemenis rejoice in their unity and are preparing to celebrate it with great enthusiasm. The flag of Yemen with its three colors reflects the people's orientation. The red color on top symbolizes our dedication to jihad for our revolution. The white color stands for our new era of peace, tranquility and freedom. Finally the black color represents the black times of isolation and backwardness. We love our country and are proud of it and will fight for our unity and freedom

Democracy is the opposite of a plug-and-play system, and many bureaucratic processes had become paralyzed. Worse. Assassinations of political figures made headlines, and within a span of weeks it had become mainstream. Assassination attempts seemed to touch all political parties, but it affected southern political figures and the Yemen Socialist Party (YSP) leaders disproportionately. This not only increased the level of political mistrust among the political elites, but also reduced the public's confidence with the newfound political system of pluralism.

"*Throughout history, no government was able to rule Yemen except through the Tribal system,*" said Sheikh Abdulwahab Sinan of the Bakil tribal confederation, when I interviewed him about the tensions in late 1991. His point was that we would have to do things the Yemeni way. We'd struggle to learn it, refine it, but we'd eventually find it.

By the first anniversary of *Yemen Times*, a degree of normalcy had begun to set in. We were finally breaking even, thanks to an increasing influx of advertising, with regular clients advertising services that catered to the diplomatic and expatriate community and Yemen's educated elite. A few tourism and hospitality advertisements, coupled with the occasional vacancy and congratulatory notices to the leadership and people on occasion of a national day or Eid celebrations, courtesy of company X or brand Y. I was happy to take in whatever to keep *Yemen Times* afloat, especially considering our volatile situation and the risks I continued to take – financially, politically, and even personally.

We celebrated the one-year anniversary with cake and a small celebratory party. I took the occasion to organize a retreat-style planning session with the *Yemen Times* team. There were four of us now in the editorial team, and a few stringers and irregular contributors who were paid by the article and the contribution. The core team at the time was Ameen Nouisser, Fatmeh Raweh, Yahia Hudeidi, and me. We divided the tasks among us any way the work demanded, often ranging from troubleshooting to building an inventory of publication-ready stories as we saw the next print deadline approaching. It was a steep learning curve, and we did what we could. In retrospect, the hardest part was proofreading as we almost always had to undertake the interviews, editorial analysis, and feature development in Arabic then translate it to English, which is a job that fell either on me or Fatmeh. We pulled through.

Nonetheless, *Yemen Times*'s survival and sustainability depended on the country's long-term stability. We need the basic governance processes to work. Things like getting a budget approved, criteria for official appointments and civil service promotion, exercising proper diplomatic protocols, and running basic services. There was no justifiable reason for the vaccination programs to pause pending political bickering between the two unification rivals. This remained a most fragile transition, and if you take a close look at day-to-day events and discourse, you would be most pessimistic.

We had many hiccups, often painful. Yet we were making progress. New legislation was passed, the noisy media was making politicians think twice. The vibrancy of political life and the back-and-forth facilitated gradual political learning toward a degree of maturity. Parliamentarians who had no idea what their jobs were, were suddenly playing a borderline-passable role in holding the executive to account. I saw this transition as a short-term pain for long-term gain.

One reason for my optimism was that democracy is cyclical. We were bound to have another round of elections, we had term limits, and we had systems to replace officials that none of our neighboring countries had. These processes were the true source of wellbeing and stability. Plus, our next parliamentary elections were in

November 1992, less than a year in the future. Things could still go wrong, but I was betting they wouldn't.

Things Going Wrong

The year 1992 was quite eventful. The factors that pushed the North and South toward unification seemed to be tearing the country apart. Hiccups in mergers between key institutions, such as the civil service, armed forces, and even the airlines seemed entrenched. Both parties to the unification – the GPC, which ruled the North, and the YSP, which ruled the South – seemed to disrespect the transitional unification roadmap, and kept on holding on to their traditional influence networks for fear the other side would take over everything. Distrust was mounting, especially of new actors that emerged in the political scene, such as the various colors of Islamist parties.

This distrust increased visibly as the parliamentary elections approached, with disagreements on how the elections would be organized and what guaranteed their integrity. Neither party seemed to prioritize the "will of the people," so to speak, but rather how to maximize its own influence. The GPC's bases were in the tribal, more populous North, which outnumbered the South three to one, and their only sizeable competition was Islah in that base. Despite being more organized, the YSP seemed unable to recruit significant support in the North due to image problems, political ideology, and limited tribal networks. In fact, it seemed that every time the YSP attempted to expand its influence in the North, it systematically backfired to benefit either the GPC or one of the Islamist parties that positioned themselves as the ideological opposites to the YSP. The collapse of the USSR and misperceptions that the YSP officials were Leninist godless heathens didn't help either.

Moving forward felt like pushing a cart with a square and a triangle for wheels. However, not moving forward was not an option as the elections were integral to both Yemen's democratic process and the legitimacy of the State. Subsequently, more time was needed as November 1992 was fast approaching, and everybody needed to prepare better, particularly the two political juggernauts, the GPC and the YSP. These two parties had much to lose from both the elections and the multiparty system, as they used to have 100% of the power in both North and South, respectively.

A six-month postponement of the elections to April 1993 might have done them both good, to organize themselves and see how they could co-opt the elections. Plus, some of the smaller political parties had shown an unexpected degree of heft, particularly Islah with its Islamist basis. A couple of other political parties had shown some potential, namely the Ba'athis, who had been active in the 1980s in the North with legacy support from Saddam and others, and a newcomer party called Al-Haq or the Truth, which had links with Iranian proxies.

Al-Haq party has a peculiar association with a small community in Sa'ada in Northern Yemen. Their story was that a Salafi religious school was established with Saudi funding in their area in the later 1970s, and local Zaydi youth started getting interested in the school and converting to Salafism. In response, some local influentials from this community reached out to Iran, seeking support to counter with their own religious school, and even went a step beyond to establish the Believing Youth Faction to counter the Salafi influence. Opening the space for everybody allowed for extremes to resurface that could spell trouble but my hope was that, as Yemen's democratic experience matured, all colors of Yemeni society would engage with one another peacefully and tacitly.

The question therefore was how democratic would it be for the two ruling parties to co-opt the process to yield the pre-Unification status quo? Not very, despite it being it their agreed plan. Their gentlemen's agreement was that they would divide the electoral map, and in many electoral districts either party would not nominate a candidate or would nominate a weak one to let the other near-guarantee their victory. This way the "real competition" would be limited to a handful of districts, probably the ones more likely to be closely watched, out of 301 districts in total.

Plus, the postponement of the elections to April 1993 gave me time to toss my own hat into the ring.

Chapter 11: Vote for Abdulaziz

Running for parliament hadn't been on my to-do list, but it was the idea of my neighbor and fellow University professor Dr Abdulghani, who himself served as a Member of Parliament for the GPC. For him, it was an easy process, as the GPC both sponsored his campaign and carried out the legwork. For me, I'd have to do it all by myself as an independent candidate. I could run in the electoral district covering my village, which happened to neighbor Dr Abdulghani's electoral unit, and he would share a few pointers with me from his experience. Sure, why not.

I could be scrappy and ran an effective shoe-string campaign. I needed a few endorsements, a logo and a motto, a campaign program, and, more importantly, a budget. As a self-financed candidate, this last point was particularly worrying, I had depleted most of my savings getting *Yemen Times* up and running. Now, just as it was borderline breaking even, I started a new adventure that I was positive – even were it to succeed – won't make financial sense. Little did I realize that the biggest challenge was getting Aziza to agree.

"*NO!*"

"*I'll do it anyway. This is my human right...*" I responded, laughingly trying to win her over.

"*You will be butting heads with much bigger heads. You know they are looking for an excuse to get rid of you,*" she responded.

"But Dr Abdulghani did it and it wasn't a big deal, just a couple of weeks campaigning..."

"Dr Abdulghani has political backing... You don't have anything," she responded

"But I have you, and you're all I need..."

I like to think that I charmed Aziza into agreeing to supporting my candidacy, but part of me thinks that she knew it was a lost battle, given how hard-headed I could be. My campaign was simple. Vote for me and I'll work for you. My slogan was actually a Quranic verse saying: *Work* [righteously]*: Soon will Allah observe your work, and His Messenger, and the Believers.* Plus, my photos in the campaign were printed in full color, unlike my competition who used black and white posters. They were more expensive, but I felt they carried a bigger impact.

My electoral district had over 200,000 residents, distributed across a series of villages and small townships. I had three teams. The first was an outreach team that would go scoping; identify locations for gatherings, like a local market, school, or other place; and gather intelligence on what the key issues were. Do they need the road fixed? Has the watering hole gone bad? This team would also identify local elders, influencers, and opinion leaders that I should meet, and then advise the second and third teams of that information. The second team would go to the recommended locations and place campaign posters, spread the word that their favorite candidate - Dr Abdulaziz Al-Saqqaf - was coming, get permissions to use the space if needed, and set up a stage and sound system, among other operational details. The third team was me. I would go shake hands warmly starting with the identified persons, deliver a passionate speech about their specific needs, mention the names of the local leaders I had just met, and say vote for me and I'll get this done for you.

The campaign was working wonderfully and I truly felt genuine connections. There was so much that needed to be done for people who were largely underserved. And the economist in me got thinking on how the costs of a palatial residence of one of the ministers or senior officials could solve most of the problems for those 200,000 or so residents in my electoral district. Yemen's developmental challenges weren't particularly expensive, they just needed a system that worked for the people.

Unbeknownst to me, the YSP candidate has complained to GPC officials in the region that my candidacy was hurting his chances, noting that this electoral unit was "promised to the YSP." Dr Abdulghani leaked this information to me, suggesting I could possibly salvage my campaign if I would agree to be a GPC ally in the parliament. It appeared that the GPC had nudged many "independent" candidates to run in YSP-allocated electoral areas to crowd-out candidates, despite their gentlemen's agreement. I told him that this isn't something I could possibly agree to. I believed in the system and I thought I had a good shot of doing this on my own.

So, the GPC sent a sabotage team to follow us everywhere we went like a shadow team. Perhaps me winning a parliamentary seat was more dangerous than the YSP, and perhaps they needed examples to show the YSP, after the elections, that they went out of their way to stick to their gentlemen's agreement. That team's job was to tell the people we just met that they had fallen victim to a scam. *Don't get fooled by Al-Saqqaf,* they would say. *He's a liar, can't deliver, has no political party backing him, and is just there to make noise.* The sabotage team was successful, and I lost the election to the YSP candidate. I've also come to understand the YSP's difficulties in recruiting new membership in the North, and why their reputation as godless heathens seemed to follow them like a shadow everywhere they went, despite them speaking to the contrary.

This was an eye-opening experience, learning about our young democracy first-hand. The GPC won 123 seats out of 301, followed by the Islah party with 62 seats, YSP with 56 seats, and 47 went to independents – most of whom joined the GPC after the elections. Another five political parties won 12 seats between them, and 13 parties won no seats. The results were particularly upsetting to the YSP, coming in third with less than half what the GPC had won. This caused havoc in post-elections political life, and the distrust became outright hostility.

Beyond my own experience, this election created new political and power dynamics as it changed the fifty-fifty power split between the two parties that unified Yemen: the GPC and the YSP. Simply put, this election guaranteed the 50% power share of the GPC, while Islah and others ate up the YSP's share in a move that looked like it was orchestrated by the GPC and friends.

Let's Talk about Lying

I'm not a sore loser but the defeat left a bitter taste in my mouth, especially since I felt that the successful candidate was undeserving. I also needed to figure out a way to rebuild my tarnished reputation of being a liar thanks to that GPC operation. I did not have to be a Member of Parliament in order to serve the people, and there was another election coming up in four years' time.

My plan was to devise some kind of a vehicle to support the local communities, thus the Hadharem Welfare Association was established. It was called Hadharem as our collective name across these villages as people who traced their lineage to the Hadhramaut region of Yemen. As its founding president, I guided the association to focus on two tasks. The first was to flag the development needs of the wider region to government and international development partners; I had done some lobbying in the 1980s to establish a groundwater pumping station this way, and I thought I could make this work to prioritize our region in future development plans. The second task was anchored in the chief complaint my team gathered during our campaigning, which was the lack of work. Young men resorted to migrating to urban locations while women eked out a living from the land and from whatever they could produce. Subsequently, the chief project for the association was to create a Women Development Center to help these women make good money, via teaching them a marketable skill.

I had studied Japan's Meiji restoration and distilled a key lesson for underdeveloped economies: in the decade following 1868, the Japanese government had built large-scale pilot economic plants, which they sold to family-based conglomerates once they became profitable. My model was to do the same, based on a collective risk-and-reward-sharing approach, through the association. Having done a feasibility study on what would work, I identified that haute couture will be our thing. We'd need to start at the basics, though. A training center, textiles and sewing machines, and lots of talent and hard work. We even had two Japanese volunteers embedded in the community to teach the necessary skills.

In parallel, I doubled down on using *Yemen Times* as a tool to verify leadership's messaging. We had to fact-check what the officials said and announced, confirm validity of claims they made, and verify numbers cited. This was critical as socioeconomic hardships continued to mount for all Yemenis, and the government's national development plans had made lots of claims, especially now as we started to produce oil in commercial quantities. Was money flowing in being spent right? More importantly, was it not getting lost to our endemic corruption?

Lies, deceptions, and half-truths are all a part of the modus operandi of political life. However, the fragility of our transition and the frustration of the masses required doing better. This wasn't about my personal vendetta; this was about making Yemen a good world citizen, and that started now, today, here.

Continuing this work with rigor meant that our growing team needed more room than our office flat by the Central bank could offer, so we found a different location facing the French embassy. It was a nice two-story building and could accommodate three more workstations as well as additional space to further grow. However, getting caught in the post-election political gridlock and power struggle meant continued harassment by the usual suspects. Soon enough our landlord forced us out due to outside pressure as he "*didn't want any trouble or troublemakers in his building.*" Eventually, we rented the basement of a large building nearby, owned by a powerful tribesman and paid a premium for it. Our new landlord wasn't easily intimidated and had his own security arrangements to deal with anyone harassing his building and its tenants. This base of operations served us well over the next few years, despite its own share of ups and downs.

I visited Prime Minister Al-Attas on a weekend Friday morning at his official residence in Sana'a and told him about our troubles. I was surprised to hear him say that he was being forced out too and his decrees are not implemented. He said that Ministers from the YSP needed to run their decisions by deputies associated with the GPC for these decisions to be enforced. He raised this issue with both President Saleh and Vice President Al-Baidh, and President Saleh asked him for a list of the officials who did not cooperate so that he would replace them. The surprising part is that the Prime Minister later learnt that the President rewarded these individuals for their insubordination with lands and other gifts from the public treasury. This was a most ominous sign for what lay ahead.

• Analysis •

I Don't Think President Ali Abdullah Saleh is Candid about Fighting Corruption. Can He Prove it? Here is a Chance!

The Permanent Committee of the People's General Congress held an exceptional meetings during 8-10/6/1993. The purpose of the meetings was to ratify the alliance document with the Yemeni Socialist Party, and the Coalition Document with the YSP and the Islah.

The Permanent Committee also used the opportunity to review the elections results and the standing of the party as compared to the others. Considerable soul-searching was also done in the three-day meetings.

But what is spectacular in all the sessions and debates was the opening address of President Ali Abdullah Saleh, Secretary-General of the PGC.

He looked the camera (and of course, the audience) straight in the eye and said, "We shall not tolerate any abuse of authority or misuse of public funds. We shall stop all corruption and corrupt individuals."

Having listened to the president utter those words, at first, I was amused. My

feelings were that it is all a lot of rhetoric. "That is the last man who should say something like that," I told myself.

A few minutes later, I began to think, "What if, just if, he meant what he said."

Suppose he wants to make real change and he needs our help.

I could not get rid of these afterthoughts.

Then came a brilliant idea - put him to the test.

A few weeks ago, the President himself had given orders to award large chunks of land to some of his proteges, such as Mutahhar Taqi, Deputy Information Minister and Chairman of the Sanaa Branch of the PGC. Mr. Abdo Boragi, Presidential Press Secretary, and others.

This was not the first time the President gives these "bribes" to his men.

The problem this time is that these men have haunted Sanaa University by slicing away its land. They eyed some prime property and wanted to take it. Their choice fell on property owned by the University.

Mr. President:
If you mean what you said, and you want me, and many other Yemenis, to believe you, please stop your men from haunting Sanaa University.

Most Yemenis are tired of empty promises. I am giving you a concrete example for you to show us that you mean what you said.

Your men, protected by a group of soldiers from a military camp commanded by one of your nearest relatives, are trying to forcibly snatch the real estate of the university. What they are doing is illegal, immoral, and outright ugly.

Mr. President:
Will you show us you are serious about what you said. We are waiting!

Prof Abdulaziz Al-Saqqaf, Sanaa University.

Chapter 12: Undemocratic Democracy

Post-election political life raised new levels of tension due to the YSP's disgruntlement with the results of the elections. President Saleh tried to send messages assuring the YSP that they would retain their role in post-election political life, and even proposed the establishment of a second parliamentary chamber dubbed Al-Shura Council with a disproportionately larger YSP representation – an issue to which Islah objected. However, YSP leadership took issue with almost everything, especially that Islah is now the second largest parliamentary block and wanted to play a bigger and more deserved role in political life than YSP.

Most of the YSP's grievances fell into three categories. The first had to do with YSP elites' issues in Sana'a, such as the diminishing role its leadership played during the transition period and general discomfort with political life in Sana'a; being the capital of unified Yemen and having its culture and practices influence governance and decision-making. Related grievances had to do with the issue of security following the assassinations of several YSP senior figures, with questions on the quality of investigation and due process. Also at issue was the quality of accommodations and facilities for newcomers from the South who were used to a more egalitarian standard of living, compared to the relative luxury of their well-established peers in Sana'a. Another was the varying degrees of respect for rule of law and tolerance for corruption, where rules were more guidelines for northerners and afternoon Qat social sessions were the go-to locations to discuss government affairs, compared to the strict interpretation of law that their southern colleagues were used to.

The second category of grievances was associated with sharp declines in the quality of life for the people in the South following unification. Part of this was due to the punishment exacted on Yemen for Saleh's position during the Iraqi invasion of Kuwait, while another had to do with the poor amalgamation of the civil service where thousands of civil servants in the South did not receive their salaries while their counterparts in the North did. Chiefly, economic mismanagement and inflation hurt everyone, but in particular the populace in the South, who had been sheltered by a socialist regime that provided them with their basic needs prior to the unification, and was now no more. It was tempting for many to associate the unification era with their socioeconomic hardship, and demand that the good old days be brought back.

The third category of grievances was on Islah, and the influence of religion in political life in general. Many ex-Marxist-Leninist YSP leaders felt uncomfortable treading in this area, while other leaders did not have the depth of knowledge or comfort to push back or diplomatically engage with such a sensitive topic, especially now that Islah was the second largest parliamentary block. One example of this was how the parliament scrapped the South's more progressive and liberal family law in favor of the North's version, on the basis of being more Islamic, to the dismay of many YSP leaders. Plus, Islah had reported ties with Saudi Arabia that gave it financial clout and a regional edge that the YSP lacked. Islah's head, Sheikh Al-Ahmar, won the coveted role of Speaker of Parliament with almost everybody but the YSP voting for him. This situation affected the YSP's relevance to the future Yemen and diminished its chances in future rounds of elections.

Unable to deal with this situation, the YSP's leadership moved back to Aden, working to re-establish the pre-unification and pre-democratization order. Vice President Al-Baidh started building the political and military base for a new State. He established contact with regimes that were enemies of Saleh and the GPC in Sana'a, and found that some of them were willing to finance his efforts to break the country. Many southerners were urged to leave Sana'a and go back to Aden, in preparation for the new country.

President Saleh and his Islah allies, in the meanwhile, announced that they would be forced to stop the break-away state. By early 1994, it was clear a war was inevitable, in spite of the best efforts of many Yemenis, as well as others, especially King Hussein of Jordan.

YEMEN TIMES

• June 6th through 12th, 1993 • Volume: III, Issue # 22 • PRICE: 10 Riyals •

Off to a shaky start...
Al-Attas' "New" cabinet paralyzed from the start, as its Islah members boycott it.

Mr. Haider Abubakr Al-Attas, Prime Minister

INSIDE THIS ISSUE

Eid Rites:
The Tides of Change
p.4

Dr. Fadhl Al-Quba
on Khalifah Hospital
in Al-Turbah
p. 9

Kuwaitis Told to
Tighten Belt
p. 14

Permanent Features:
• Review of Local Press: p. 6

• Letters to the Editor: p. 8

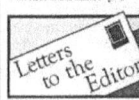
• French Pages 10 + 11

• English Lessons: p.: 15

Quality Motor Oils
CALTEX

The names of the "new" Al-Attas government have been read over the radio and television, and the papers have printed them. Yet, the Al-Attas government hit a snag - the Islah members refused to take the constitutional oath and start their job. Their complaint - they want at least an equal share to the YSP.

"We can't amend the government even before it starts its functions," a senior PGC politician told a senior Islah politician trying to convince him to show flexibility. "Why not, we are amending the constitution even before it is implemented," retorted the Islah person.

Yemen Times learned that there will not amendments to the government, but the leadership will make it up for the Islah in distributing posts of deputy ministers and chairmen of government companies and corporations. On the basis of that understanding, the Islah has agreed to play the game.

In the "new" cabinet, twelve persons occupy their same posts as in the previous Attas government, six of them have rotated jobs, and six former ministers have returned to the "new" government. The real doze of new blood comes, understandably, from the Islah bloc which has never ruled before. Even then, both the PGC and YSP have together introduced three new faces.

One observer who was shocked as he was reading the names, said, "The political leadership has expressed a definite longing for the past. You can see this in the structure of the 'new' government."

This situation has made many people conclude that this was a temporary government. Their logic - once the constitution is amended, and the presidency is re-structured, and Ali Abdullah Saleh and Ali Salem Al-Beedh are named by the House of Representatives as president and vice president, then another "new" government will be formed.

The process in this scenario has already been set in motion, and the works are in the pipeline. Remaining time for the completion of the jobless than five months.

This kind of psychological frame leads to more hesitation and paralysis as a new transitional period mentality grips the system. "By giving the presidency a five-month extension, the parliament has actually initiated a new transitional period," pointed out a Sanaa University Professor. "This is bad for the country which needs a decisive and firm leadership which can lead us out of the current mess," he added.

What happens next? Nothing meaningful or substantial as President Ali Abdullah Saleh continues to juggle more and more balls at the same time. As the number of balls rises, the pace of the system slows down. Even if there is no mishap, the system may grind to a halt under the weight of its contradictions.

Meanwhile, the economic difficulties continue to mount. As the price spiral eats away on the purchasing power of the people, grievances will be expressed in more violent ways.

The few days preceding the Eid Al-Adha witnessed major demonstrations in Sanaa. The army and riot police was called in to disperse an angry crowd of civil servants. It used tear gas and clubs and fired shots in the air. In the end, an inefficient bureaucracy was forced to work over the weekend to pay salaries.

There was also trouble in the army as many of them became edgy for not receiving their salaries on time. The Mareb barracks saw heated arguments and low-level violence between the rank and file and the officers. The president had to go there immediately after the Eid to pacify the soldiers.

***

Members of the "New" Al-Attas Cabinet

YSP Members:			
1. Haider Abubakr Al-Attas	Prime Minister	Same Person, Same Post, Last Gov't
2. Mohammed Haidarah Masdoos	Vice Prime Minister	Same Person, Same Post, Last Gov't
3. Haitham Qasim Taher	Minister of Defense	Same Person, Same Post, Last Gov't
4. Saleh Abu Bakar Bin Husseinoon	Minister of Oil & Mineral Resources	Same Person, Same Post, Last Gov't
5. Rashid Mohsin Alsamidi	Minister of Fisheries	Informing Post, Last Gov't
6. Saleh Obaid Ahmed	Minister of Transportation	Same Person, Different Post, Last Gov't
7. Mohammed Saeed Abdullah	Minister of Housing	Same Person, Same Post, Last Gov't
8. Izedin Omar	Minister of Culture	Same Person, Different Post, Last Gov't
9. Mohammed Al Qadi	Minister of Electricity & Water	New Blood
10. Ahmed A. Salmeen		

PGC Members:			
1. Dr. Yassin Mohammed Saeed	First Vice Prime Minister	Same Person, Same Post, Last Gov't
2. Dr. Mohammed Saeed Al-Attar	Deputy Prime Minister/Foreign Minister	Same Person, Same Post, Last Gov't
3. Abdel Al Salami	Minister of Finance	Same Person, Same Post, Last Gov't
4. Abdullah Al-Kurshumi	Minister of Public Works	Same Person, Same Post, Last Gov't
5. Dr. Mohammed Al-Kabab	Minister of Youth & Sports	Same Person, Same Post, Last Gov't
6. Najeeb Hamza Abu Ras	Minister of Legislation	Same Person, Same Post, Last Gov't
7. Ahmed Mohammed Al-Ansi	Minister of Communications	Same Person, Same Post, Last Gov't
8. Hassan Al Lowzy	Minister of Information	Same Person, Same Post, Last Gov't
9. Dr. Ismail Taha Al-Mutawakkel	Minister of Tourism	Same Person, Same Post, Other Gov't
10. Dr. Abdel Karem Al-Iryani	Minister of Planning	Same Person, Same Post, Other Gov't
11. Abdullah Hussein	Minister of Justice	Same Person, Same Post, Other Gov't
12. Mohammed Ba-Sindwah	Minister of Foreign Affairs	Same Person, Diff post Post, Other Gov't
13. Yahya Shalialan	Minister of Civil Service	Same Person, Different Post, Other Gov't
14. Dr. Mohammed Ali Badwan	Minister of State Security	Same Person, Different Post, Other Gov't
15. Dr. Abdullah Al Qabi	Minister of Education	New Blood

Islah Members:			
1. Abdulwahab Al Ansi	Deputy Prime Minister	New Blood
2. Mohammed Yadomi	Minister of Local Government	New Blood
3. Dr. Najeeb Ghanem	Minister of Health	New Blood
4. Dr. Ghaleb Abdul Adil Qassim	Minister of Endowment (Awqaf)	New Blood
5. Dr. Abdul Wahab Al-Dailami	Minister of Supply	New Blood
6. Ahmed Salem Rajah Kurman	Minister of Legal Parliamentary Affairs	New Blood

Other:			
1. Mujahid Abu Shawareb	Vice Prime Minister	Same Person, Same Post, Last Gov't

*Gov't = Government
*Last = Last Al-Attas Government
Other = Pre Al-Attas Government

BTT TRAVEL & TOURISM
BAZARA TRAVEL & TOURISM
NDASAD CARGO EXPRESS
☐ INTERNATIONAL/LOCAL CHARTERS
☐ PACKING/FORWARDING BY AIR/SEA/LAND
☐ CUSTOMS CLEARANCE, DOOR-TO-DOOR SERVICE
Sana'a: Phone: 205-925/865, Telex: 2598; Fax: 209-568

YEMEN GENERAL INSURANCE CO. (S.Y.C.)
WE INSURE
Motor, Marine, Fire, Life+Personal Accident, Contractors all risks, burglary, Workmen compensation
BRANCHES
Sana'a: Tel: 265191 - Fax: 263109
Aden - Tel: 02-241909 - Taiz: 04-221561
Hodeidah Tel: 03-239184 - Fax: 211576

BAZARA CORPORATION
Travel & Tourism
GSA: KLM Royal Dutch Airlines
BAZ TOURS
Tour Operators
Phone: 272143/270879/76968/275021
Fax: 967-1-270880
687ubciry St. P. O. Box (12519) - Sanaa

ARAMEX
We Hit Your Target
Anywhere in the Globe
Sana'a - Tel: 243925 - Fax: 240794,
Aden - Tel: 255683, 253952 - Taiz - Tel: 213489,
Hodeidah - Tel: 218168-218675

EL SOFFARY

Yemen's Only English-Language Newspaper

• June 13th through 19th, 1993 • Volume: III, Issue # 23 • Price: 10 Riyals •

Sheikh Abdullah Bin Hussain Al–Ahmar to Yemen Times:

"I don't believe the country needs the proposed Al-Shura Council."

Dr. Abdulaziz Al-Saqqaf, Chief Editor in an interview with Sheikh Al-Ahmar, Speaker of Parliament

INSIDE

Childbirth in Yemen: Primitive Services p.4

The PGC-YSP-Islah Agreement p.5

Al-Mikhlafi Comments on the Elections p. 7

A Challenger for the Presidency? p. 12

The Dutch Pledge Continued Aid. p. 14

Permanent Features:
• Review of Local Press: p.6

• Letters to the Editor: p. 8

Yemen and Kuwait Inch Towards Each Other:

FIRST HIGH LEVEL KUWAITI-YEMENI OFFICIAL MEETING...

to the new Yemeni Minister, Mohamed Ba-Sindiwah, the of Yemen and the State of Kuwait, are closer to each other, going to see my counterpart, Sheikh Al-Ahmad, on June 23 in Geneva," Ba-sh said in what prom-be the first official between the two following the Iraqi of Kuwait in 1989.

At another level, a Kuwaiti press delegation arrived in Sanaa on Thursday, June 10th, and interviewed President Ali Abdullah Saleh on Friday, a usual holiday. The group also saw the Foreign and Information Ministers.
Foreign Minister Ba-Sindiwah had earlier told Kuwait's As-Styasah newspaper that he was chosen for the job given his close and warm relations with Kuwait and the Gulf.

Exclusive for:
Yemen Times

Sheikh Abdullah Bin Hussain Al-Ahmar, the Speaker of Parliament, the Chairman of the Yemeni Congregation for Reform (Islah), and the paramount Sheikh of Hashed, has forced the government to undergo a reshuffle even before it takes office. "We have agreed on five seats for the Islah in a 24-person government. Now we will

> "The Islah agrees to be under-represented in government at this stage to ensure harmonious and peaceful evolution."

pick up two more portfolios," he told the Yemen Times in an exclusive interview.

When asked about what he thought of the preparations to establish the Al-Shura Council (Senate), the Sheikh said he did not believe the country needed one more forum for mindless and unnecessary arguments.
With respect to the scramble of political parties to support the demands for local rule and decentralization in Yemen, Sheikh Al-Ahmar broke off from the main line of reasoning and described such efforts as political expediency and verbose. "This country does not even have a strong and effective central government. So what power is to be parcelled off to pass on to local authorities? What we need is to straighten out our administrative and financial procedures so that decisions can be taken in the various governorates without need for referral to the central government," Sheikh Al-Ahmar explained.
In explaining the small share of the Islah party in government when compared to the other two parties, specially the YSP, Sheikh Al-Ahmar stated that his party is interested in the harmonious and peaceful evolution of the political system of Yemen.
"Towards that objective, we agree to be under-

represented in the executive branch of authority. We do not see that we need to be in the forefront of the implementation process, provided that what is being implemented is agreed upon," he added.
"The two priority issues that the new government must address are the economic and security concerns of citizens. Without visible results on those two fronts, we can't expect real progress," Sheikh Al-Ahmar concluded.

> "The calls for local rule and decentralization are simply lots of political verbiage. Yemen doesn't even have an effective central government."

Read full details on page 9

Chapter 12: War

Outmaneuvered politically, the YSP found itself an orphan in the world, and wanted to escape the only way it knew how – forward, and violently if needed. The other side was happy to oblige, and in fact took initiative with inflammatory remarks that were matched with military escalation on the ground.

Islah also had its grievances. It started its political career by giving away concessions; it looked like the political process had a double standard, where it got half as many cabinet positions than YSP, despite winning more parliamentary seats. President Saleh pulled strings to keep the process going, buying favors here, co-opting others there, forging new alliances and creating new frenemies. His decision to take this on was perhaps necessary given his role as President and grand patron of the political process, but it also isolated his unification partner who staged his second strike in late 1993 and retreated to Aden. Vice President Al-Baidh listed eighteen demands to end his strike, which were incorporated into a reconciliation agreement brokered by His Majesty King Hussein of Jordan. That agreement never had a chance to be realized.

President Saleh and his Islah allies, in the meanwhile, announced that they would be forced to stop Al-Baidh's efforts to create the break-away State. By early 1994, it was clear a war was inevitable. The reconciliation agreement brokered by King Hussein included provisions to centralize control of the armed forces under the respective ministries and do away with the split loyalties. This had been a pending issue throughout the transitional period, discussed in the cabinet, in parliament, and in mediations to de-escalate political tensions, including through constitutional and legal reforms.

These were unprecedentedly difficult times in the age of the young republic, where the GPC, although it had the most influence, also feared the YSP for never conceding the South's army under a unified command. Furthermore, the YSP also had influence in the South through its traditional rank-and-file membership. Islah had its own strengths vis-a-vis the GPC, such as its ability to split the northern population between itself and the GPC, having regional backers with deep pockets, and a cunning ability to use religious discourse for its own devices. The GPC didn't need any more competition or foes; it needed to regain control.

One strategy was to empower smaller parties to do to the YSP and the Islah what these two parties were trying to do to the GPC. The small parties would help create splits within the major parties and contest their messaging and mandates. Yemen already had some twenty political parties, and some of the smaller were poised for that role. Perhaps more chaos would be one way of dealing with the current political deadlock. Surely, YSP, Islah, and others had their own calculations as well. President Saleh was quick to inflame the tensions, with skirmishes between battalions affiliated to both regimes in the North and South taking place, eventually leading to an armed confrontation against a southern battalion located in Amran on April 27, 1994, followed with a retaliatory air bombardment by the South's air force on Sana'a, and a full-scale war by May 5th.

It was a quick but devastating war that lasted the better part of three months, causing over 10,000 casualties and unspeakable horrors. The war was also a propaganda and ideology war, with the GPC/Islah machine working unexpectedly effectively against any messaging that came from the YSP leadership. It had succeeded in splitting the YSP, matching the moral higher ground with significant brute-force presence on the ground. Northern army units encircled southern units stationed in the North and asked them to either join them in the war against the secessionists or surrender immediately. Many southern commanders stationed in the North decided not to fight, though the southern forces that fled to the North following the 1986 civil war in the South did. The secessionist regime did not have the same success in encircling northern units stationed in the South.

Yemen Times accompanied the conflict, deployed more stringers, and reported on it diligently as it continued publishing every week. We extensively documented everything we knew and found out through first-hand sources on the ground, and contrasted that with the official statements issued by both parties. Our commitment to truth was unwavering as was necessary in times like those. At the height of the war, *Yemen Times* was printed using a manual screen offset printer and distributed via bicycles when we had fuel and electricity crises. We had our team live and work in the *Yemen Times* offices to deal with the curfew and security situation. Even Aziza and the kids moved into the office to help as much as they could. The show must go on.

Yemen Times's record of the conflict had some important differences from what the Sana'a authorities reported. *Yemen Times* investigation on the battle that started the war in Amran on April 27th found out that it was indeed started by troops of the northern-affiliated First Armed Division, headed by Ali Muhsen Al-Ahmar. They started the war by attacking the southern-affiliated Third Armored Division, not too far from its location. We also published casualty figures, both military and civilian, that were higher than what the government claimed. We worked with other investigative journalists to verify these numbers through recruitment offices, volunteer lists, and even battle-to-battle body counts. We also engaged with military experts to help us understand and validate official statements. Often a statement would come out saying that 250 were killed and another 500 wounded in military camp so and so, which we knew had 3,000 troops in it as of the last count just weeks back. The remaining troops didn't just disappear, especially as that camp was fully mobilized and at a high degree of preparedness ahead of the battle.

At one point, when the government claimed to have downed a southern air force plane, we asked for a location or coordinates. We followed the given coordinates in search of this wreckage to take a picture; no wreckage was found, and it looked like it was a hoax. To keep us silent, I and six fellow journalists were abducted, beaten, insulted, and tortured. I recall hearing the fingers of my colleagues break and was told my fingers would be next. Luckily, I escaped the worst of that episode, but it still haunts me.

I had several such prior experiences with different parts of the government. A year into *Yemen Times*'s life, I was sued by the Ministry of Information for publishing false information, which turned out to be a translation error on their part and a public embarrassment for them. I also received notes threatening me, and bullet holes in my car's driver door. I had been called into the security apparatus for extended interviews, and held for a few days under investigation. But those were in times of peace, where I had some recourse. Being abducted in the middle of a war was a different story.

As the war ended, July 7th was declared victory day. President Saleh accused the *Yemen Times* and *Al-Ayyam* newspapers of dubious practices, saying that he was directing an early warning to us because the Minister of Information was hesitant to take legal measures against both institutions. The President further told Al-Sharq Al-Awsat that he would "*take the appropriate measures at the appropriate time.*"

After a brief respite, I came back to my usual self. Luckily the war was over, and I had some catching up to do. The week after, I published an editorial reiterating that I still thought the country's leaders believed in freedom of the press, and I listed seven reasons why I thought President Saleh won this war. My article didn't mention anything unknown, but it was a message that Al-Saqqaf was still there and would continue to do what he did in service of democracy and human rights in Yemen.

They got my message. I know they got my message because they told me so, saying that they welcomed my positive messaging and recommended that I continue to toe the line, warning me of more consequences if I didn't. I called a few journalist colleagues and asked if they received similar threats, which they had. We held a meeting at the *Yemen Times* the next day to see how we could deal with this situation and build mechanisms to help us deal with a more authoritarian tone following the war. We needed to push for an end to the State of Emergency that accompanied the war, as it suspended many freedoms and protections. We also needed to revive the role of the Yemeni Journalists Syndicate and create a fund to help offset many of the legal costs and medical care expenses more and more newspapers and journalists were incurring. We must fight back, I persisted.

Reconciliation

The week after, *Yemen Times* organized a media symposium around the future of Yemen after the war. I had two goals for this event: the first was to work with media colleagues on building a mature narrative that looked beyond the pain of the war and toward the future that asserted our constitutional freedoms; the second was to show unwavering commitment toward freedom of the press and democracy. It was in times like these that we needed to step up and showcase that Yemen's democracy was still alive and well, and our role as journalists was to help recover and find our way toward the tomorrow of pluralism and prosperity that we all aspired to.

The symposium took place on July 17, 1994, at the Sana'a Sheraton Hotel, one of the few venues well equipped with a decent lunch menu for the participants. We had extended invitations to around forty journalists and editors from across the political spectrum and had the *Yemen Times* team call them to confirm their participation, which was essential for a well-informed discussion that reflected views from across political divides. We had thirty-three confirmations – including from the GPC, Islah, YSP, independents, as well as a few correspondents of regional and international media who were in Sana'a covering the war and post-war realities. After waiting for thirty minutes or so beyond the official starting time, we realized that the journalists from the GPC and Islah would probably not show – despite confirming. There were around twenty of us or so present, so we decided to start.

Following the opening, several papers were presented by myself and experts in their respective areas, such as Ahmed Al-Soufi Director of the Yemeni Institute for Development of Democracy, and Izz Aldin Al-Asbahi from The Writers Guild, among others. The discussions were lively, despite the lack of participation from our GPC and Islah colleagues, noting that we were also treading in the dark not knowing the views of those two entities. It was expected that the different parties were trying to carve out as much space for themselves in post-war Yemen as possible, with the GPC arbitrating for this power struggle and slicing out space for others. The southern representatives who had sided against the YSP leadership realized quickly that they were neither able nor allowed to fully occupy the space that the YSP left behind.

For its part, Islah expected more rewards in the political space, given the decisive role they played during the war. Nevertheless, President Saleh pushed back saying, "*The YSP is part of the political actors on the Yemeni scene, and it will continue to be so.*" Nonetheless, Islah remained keen on expanding its political influence as much as it could, even if it was at the expense of friends and allies, including the GPC. According to a Nasserite party journalist who took part in the session, it made sense for the YSP leftovers to regroup and build a broad opposition coalition to keep the GPC in check.

Whatever the stand of any party, the buzzword in Sana's political circles these days was reconciliation. This meant that the various parties recognized their differences, built their alliances, and interacted with each other within a functioning pluralist political system.

But there were other views as well, where reconciliation could also mean a broad-based government that included everybody might be an option, although it might not be in the best interests of the country's democracy since there won't be any meaningful opposition left. The majority believed that the government that could best serve the political evolution of Yemen was one formed by the GPC alone, although some felt that the GPC had expanded significantly, and its centralized decision-making around President Saleh did not evolve to reflect its growing base. Overall, there was a lot of evolution needed in the system, within the players, and for the broader geopolitical ecosystem for a democratic post-war Yemen.

The symposium represented a breath of fresh air for all of us. We felt the country was moving forward, that we were moving forward. It also was an opportunity to further develop a spirit of comradery among us journalists, over lunch, and got us touching on the steps to revive the Yemeni Journalists Syndicate. We parted ways in the early afternoon, I went back to the office to start the write-up on the symposium and attend to the day's business. Like in a normal day.

But this wasn't a normal day.

Mohammed Al-Sourmi, the Deputy Chief of the Political Security Organization, gave instructions to round up many journalists and intellectuals and lock them up. The soldiers and intelligence officers came by the dozens, at night, in civilian clothes, and swarmed houses violently, publicly, and tactlessly. I was one of twenty-two persons arrested and tortured, and almost everyone who participated in the symposium was rounded up as well.

They came at night to my home, violently knocked on my door, barged into the apartment, dragged me out and into the unmarked SUV. My daughter Haifa saw this horror. Our phone line was cut so there isn't anyone she could call. She took my phonebook, knocked at my neighbor's house, Dr Abdulghani, and said:

"They took my father. Can I use your phone?"

Haifa called everyone in my phone address book. Literally everyone, including folks I hadn't been in touch with for years. If the name had a title under it that said Ambassador, Official, or Colonel, then she called them first.

"My Father was kidnapped. Armed men came by and took him, please help, call someone. Bring me back my Father," she would say.

They put me in a 1.5 x 2.5 meter underground cell at the installations of the political security compound off Djibouti street. There was a small pad with a two-inch thick sponge to serve as my bed. No free access to the toilet, barely any light, and one piece of inedible dry bread (Kudam). That was only the beginning of the nightmare, with the sounds of agony and torment flowing through the cells over the night.

In the morning I began to inquire with my neighbors. There was Saleh Al-Baidhani, an electrician who has been in jail for over two weeks. Then there was the man from Shabwah who was accused of being a Saudi agent. And Khaled, across the hall. I didn't get a chance to know them well because it was forbidden to speak to each other. One of my neighbors persistently and recurrently asked for the time. "*What time is it?*" Then fifteen minutes later, he would ask again, "*What time is it?*" Another neighbor kept praying to God and pleading. Another kept begging for a cigarette, and so on.

In the afternoon, I was blindfolded and handcuffed, my hands behind my back. I was led by several men through a number of corridors within the building, and then pushed into a corner. Then they started beating me with their rifles and kicking me with their heavy boots. They yelled insults as they beat me.

Then they took me back to my cell, and the handcuffs were giving me a lot of pain. My wrist began to bleed. I pleaded with them to take off the blindfolds and handcuffs. First, they took off the blindfold, and then, two hours later, they took off the handcuffs. Around ten o'clock or so, they came back for me. They blindfolded me again and led me through a number of stairs and alleyways and into the back of an SUV. There were about six men. They drove for about twenty minutes, and then they told me that they would pass me on to another team. Finally, the car stopped and they helped me out. They told me to sit on the ground with my blindfolds on and wait for the pick-up team.

I waited for a while, nobody came. I heard no movement and I wondered if I was being watched. I gathered some courage to peak through the blindfolds and quickly turned them back on. Soon, I heard some barking that sounded rather menacing. I took off the blindfolds to discover that I was in the outskirts of Sana'a in the middle of a field, and with no one around. I looked around and walked toward two small houses. I knocked on the door of one of them, quickly introduced myself as a university professor, and explained that I was kidnapped by some thieves and left on that spot.

I discovered that I was in the area of Madhbah at the edge of town. They helped me to some water and asked me if I wanted to spend the night, but I cleaned up myself and sought directions back to town.

I walked for about fifteen minutes toward the main highway, and then onward toward Sana'a, wondering, all the time if the other security team would catch up with me. I hitchhiked a ride with a truck driver, and, once in Sana'a, got a taxi that brought me to the Taj Sheba Hotel, where I booked a room for the night.

I called up Dr Siyamend Othman, who was in Yemen for a brief mission, staying at the Taj and asked to see him. He kindly woke up and welcomed me to his room. Along with his colleague. Dr Abdul-Hussain Aziz, they listened to me patiently, and gave as much comfort as they could. They explained to me that there were other persons arrested as well. Since I did not know whether I was let go, or whether I was a fugitive, Dr Othman then suggested we swap rooms and asked me to sleep in his room. Dr Aziz stressed that I was to hit the wall of his next-door room in case there were any developments. Those two colleagues helped a lot to ease my mind.

The next day, I paid a quick visit to my office. I learnt that two *Yemen Times* clerks were also taken in for twenty-four hours, and they underwent a similar experience. My archives, papers, and documents were ransacked. They went through my ledgers and account books. They disconnected all my telephones, including those of my home and those of my brother-in-law. I got in touch with many individuals and groups. Everybody was horrified and shocked. No one could understand what could be achieved from such action. Many people kept wondering whether this incident set the pace and tone for the future of political interaction.

Members of the President's office kept insisting he did not know about it, and once he did, he ordered the release of everybody. Even then, not everybody was released. Meanwhile, many of the victimized journalists and politicians, members of the opposition, members of parliament, and even certain members of the government were asking for an investigation to determine who was behind the crack-down and for what purpose. This was an all-around stupid political blunder at a time when reconciliation was the rhetoric.

Haifa's campaign created so much buzz so early on that the officers who kidnapped me from the Political Security Office didn't know what to do with me. They needed to off-load me to someone else but none of the other officers wanted anything to do with me. Still at the Taj Sheba Hotel, I instructed my office to organize a press conference at the hotel, invite diplomats, the media, and everyone else who mattered. At 4pm, my press statement was brief.

"Officers from the Political Security Office kidnapped me two days ago at 10pm from my home. They terrorized my family, blindfolded me, beat me, and abandoned me outside Sana'a. Should anything happen to me or to Yemen Times, I accuse this man..." [pointing to the picture of President Saleh hung at the room].

Chapter 13: Hello, Mr President

My ordeal landed me a surprise rendezvous with President Saleh. It was sudden and brief, and I didn't have time to prepare at all, although I did expect some sort of a reaction to my press conference. He asked me about my health and family. He regretted what happened to me, but moved on to mention my recent editorial that listed seven reasons on why he won the war. He said that there was also an eighth reason. He explained that it was Al-Baidh's proclamation of the Democratic Republic of Yemen on May 21st that sealed the outcome of the war. Had Al-Baidh not done that, stuck to the agreements, and perhaps remained in Yemen somewhere inaccessible like Socotra Island, it would've been a different story.

"Mr President, you called me here to tell me just that?" I inquired, expecting him to tell me something about what had just happened to me.

"Ya Doctor, you are an educated and enlightened man. We're about to open a new page in Yemen's history, and we need patriotic people like you to help us rebuild Yemen," he replied. *"Go with God,"* he added, waving me out.

I had reached out to him personally many times directly and through the pages of *Yemen Times* asking for his intervention on various topics, and I also reached out to his office separately asking for an interview. I hoped my first encounter with him would be during more amicable times, but perhaps those amicable times were about to start? In any case, I was very happy to see that he was getting my messages and that he was a *Yemen Times* reader.

Had the war changed President Saleh? Had he become more mature, and now, as the victor, able to calm down and focus on being a good leader despite the old ways of people like Al-Sourmi and the Political Security Office? He was right that Yemen could use all the help it could get. We all had a lot of healing to do and fences to mend as well – especially with our neighbors in the region – on the road to becoming a good world citizen.

And the good news kept on coming. Not only was oil production increasing significantly, but the discovery of commercial quantities of natural gas was an added bonus. Perhaps Yemen could finally stand on its two feet and fund its own development?

A few months after the war ended, it looked like the conflict wasn't over yet. Clashes at the border with Saudi Arabia were an alarming sign, followed by the Eritrean occupation of Yemen's Hunaish islands in the Red Sea. I wrote to President Saleh, via another editorial, saying that the Eritreans were proxies trying to open a new war front, and it was best that he adopt a diplomatic approach in resolving all of Yemen's conflicts with our neighbors. He heeded my call and formed a joint committee with the Saudis to organize a dialogue on border demarcation, and resorted to international mediation to regain the Hunaish islands peacefully a couple of years later.

Better yet, through a State visit to France in early 1995, President Saleh impressed the key investor in Yemen's natural gas project, and followed that with another visit to Saudi Arabia. Yemen also received many foreign officials and diplomats at this time, including the UN Secretary-General, and it looked like the new version of unified Yemen was the version accepted by the international community. The surge of diplomacy was accompanied by a new package of multilateral development aid to help rebuild Yemen's shattered economy, with some painful but necessary IMF reforms.

Saleh also had a few tricks up his sleeve. Yemen had tried unsuccessfully to join the UK's commonwealth, noting the history of Aden in the British Empire; continued to strengthen its role in regional and global politics; and tried to join the Gulf Cooperation Council (GCC). It was vital for Yemen to rebuild its ties with both the rich neighboring countries of the gulf, as well as our neighbors in the horn of Africa. Stronger links to the region and the world would make it easier for Yemen to achieve its development goals, build for enduring stability, and strengthen the legitimacy of the post-war governing regime.

Ironically, Yemen's requests to join the Commonwealth and the GCC were both turned down due to Yemen's democratization and human rights efforts. The first for being too little, and the second for being too much. The 1997 Edinburgh Communique of the Commonwealth Heads of Governments refused Yemen's application for membership, citing ineligibility given the record on democracy and human rights. On their part, GCC concerns around Yemen were many, including Yemen's democratic governance structure, which would make it an incompatible oddity among the GCC countries.

Progress isn't always linear. Despite the comprehensive amnesty for all that was intended to help Yemen get past the wounds of war, the space for human rights and freedom of the press continued to oscillate. Those who were perceived to side with the YSP paid a heavy price, while others were either rewarded or put under further scrutiny. Perhaps what shielded *Yemen Times* was the language barrier, it was never intended to be a mass-market medium engaging with the populace, and by the time the Security apparatus translated the newspaper and got the gist of our reporting, they would've already moved on to the next topic of the day. Many of my Arabic-language fellow journalists and newspapers weren't so lucky.

The National Press Club Award

In March 1995, I was invited to Washington, DC to receive the 1995 International Freedom of the Press Award, citing our journalism during the 1994 civil war. It was a moment of great honor to be recognized by such an esteemed body, and I accepted the award on behalf of all those working for press freedom in Yemen and the region, and in service of truth. This was my acceptance speech:

Thank you very much. I'm overwhelmed.

I'd like to tell you that I come from a very small village from Yemen, I was the first-born son in my father's family and I was destined to be a bricklayer, like my father. In our tradition, the first-born son has to follow in the father's profession. As I grew up, something beautiful happened to me: the American government gave me a Fulbright scholarship. It broke that cycle, and I was finally a graduate from Harvard University. It is a big change in my life.

Today, this recognition will add another twist, a positive twist, another change to my life, and I hope, to the life of all my colleagues in my country as well as the region.

I am extremely grateful. I believe that my country will prosper only if it becomes a good world citizen and that's what I try to do, through the little I can. And I'm happy to note that my country is moving along this direction. For the last four years we have been doing a lot to democratize the country, to move toward pluralism, liberal politics, and market economics. We have our ups and downs. I have myself suffered from the downs. But I'd also like to use this moment to give credit to my own country for the many ups in our recent history.

Thank you all for everything.

The recognition reverberated in the Yemeni media, and it gave a morale boost to *Yemen Times* staff and to the journalism community. It meant the world was watching what was going on in Yemen. It meant that we were being heard, and the world cared about Yemen. I have always maintained to my students at Sana'a University and to the *Yemen Times* readership that there is a big world out there. Don't be like frogs in the bottom of a water well, fighting over whatever nothing that gets dropped into the well. There is a big world out there outside this well and you must learn about it, connect with it, and belong to the wider world community, not just your fellow frogs at the bottom of the well.

Perhaps that isn't the best metaphor to get the point across, but I sincerely hope it worked.

Democracy, Shaped by War

Post-war realities gave the GPC the impression it could renege on commitments made to democracy. So I worked with like-minded colleagues across the political spectrum to see how we could push back and assert our democratic gains; Ahmed Al-Soufi had just put together an ambitious program for the Yemeni Institute for the Development of Democracy (YIDD), to which he asked us to contribute; Nasr Taha Mustafa established the Yemeni Center for Strategic Studies and Izz Al-Din Al-Asbahi the Human Rights Information and Training Institute; Hisham BaSharahil shared ambitious plans to establish the Independent Journalists Committee to create a non-partisan space for independent journalists who were partial to democratic development. It looked like, despite the odds, the post-war era would shape its own destiny at the hands of pioneers like these.

Yemen Times also had a role to play, not only covering the various events and engagements organized by civil society partners, but also raising the bar on what needed to be said. For instance, YIDD organized a symposium on democracy and economic policy, where impediments to creating a durable democracy in Yemen would limit investments with a long-term horizon. The key message was that no investor would make a large investment that expected to yield its results after ten years, if he isn't sure that the governance framework would be consistent during that time to allow the business to continue as planned. This conclusion must link to another event's outcomes relating to rule of law showing how democratic development needed to link to both.

A problem we often faced was that the Political Security Organization (PSO) agents who attended these events did not have the sensibility to understand if what was said was good or bad. An agent would sit in the back in the room, trying to identify key words and who said them, so if a suspected opposition or independent intellectual said "democracy," then it was bad, but if it was said by a government official or GPC leader, then it is good. They had a difficult task, for which they were unqualified. I would sometimes go find them and explain to them what is going on so that their reporting was more accurate, for whatever it may have been worth.

"*Slowly slowly ya Doctor.... So what Dr Al-Maitami said was good?*" The PSO agent asked. "*If it was good, I need not mention it in my report,*" he added.

"*Son, did you understand what he said? The gist of his paper is that it would be difficult for Yemen to build an industry if private investors feel that the system of laws would not protect their investments, and so they resort to transactional commerce such as brokerages, property investment, and speculation, which do not give us an industry that can grow in perpetuity,*" I would explain.

Sometimes I would have a few of the attendees join these side conversations as we would discuss what the PSO agent would report, as he was doing his job after all, and sometimes ask good questions, such as what democracy has to do with business. I would reply, "*Everything*," and go on to explain the links.

Yemen was a least-developed country that had just come out of a war. We had a way to go. This wasn't just the beginning, it was the beginning of the beginning, but the good news was that those events were attracting more participation, including senior officials keen to engage on building the Yemen we aspired to. That, however, meant change, and resistance to change, especially by those who prioritized their own illegitimate interests over the country's wellbeing. Those, I've come to know, were many in our ruling elite. *Yemen Times* repeatedly published investigative reports about corruption, such as the head of the publicly owned Yemen Drug Company donating company funds to the GPC, or land grabs by officials who would then sell it to both public and private entities, imposing illegitimate royalties and fees on Yemeni and foreign businesses, not to mention the long list of scandals associated with oil concessions or the Aden Free Zone.

Our perseverance upset many who were benefiting from such corruption, many of whom had the ear of President Saleh. On July 7, 1996, President Saleh named me and *Yemen Times* among those who acted against Yemen's best interests. This was the second time he used this anniversary to publicly accuse me and *Yemen Times* of this, the first time in 1994. The President and those around him knew that this wasn't true, it was perhaps the lack of a sound argument or a justifiable reason to discredit me that forced them to resort to these tactics. Or perhaps he'd become annoyed with *Yemen Times*'s constant barraging for accountability, including *Yemen Times* edition of June 17th, which had an anecdote on President Al-Hamdi's drive for accountability, which probably antagonized President Saleh further against me and *Yemen Times*.

The story was that President Al-Hamdi was visiting a hospital, and ordered one of his officials to distribute a gift of ten Riyals to each of the patients in the hospital. The President sent another staffer a short while later to confirm that indeed the ten Riyals were distributed. When he was informed that the official pocketed half of that money and distributed only five Riyals, he became furious and had a public trial for that official, and was quoted saying, "*I don't want thieves around me.*" Which was a great contrast to the thieves amassing around President Saleh. In that same edition, *Yemen Times* published a full-page color portrait of President Ibrahim Al-Hamdi as a gift to its readers, as we often capitalized on space in *Yemen Times*'s color pages to include posters that the readers would cut down and post on their walls.

هدية صحيفة يمن تايمز

الشهيد ابراهيم محمد الحمدي

July 15th, 1996

Clarifying the President's Accusations

The President Openly Threatens Yemen Times and Its Editor

In his press conference on 7/7/1996, President Ali Abdullah Saleh accused the Yemen Times and its editor of shady contacts with the outside world. He explicitly accused both of being paid agents giving out wrong information to 'damage the nation's interests'.
"I am giving my warning. This is my last warning!" the President said menacingly. He finally said that he will see to it that the newspaper is printed out of Cyprus, implying that the newspaper and its editor will be pushed out of the country into exile.
(The President's full press conference is available with the newspaper on tape).

This development has resulted in a grave and dangerous situation for the Yemen Times, its editor, and the staff. The President's accusations and threats have complicated our lives, to say the least.
Following long consultations with friends, the editor decided to send a letter to the President. The original letter is reproduced next to this article, and the exact translation is given below:

Quote:

His Excellency General Ali Abdullah Saleh,
President of the Republic, Esq.,

Greetings.

I seize the occasion of the 7th of July, and forthcoming occasion of 17th of July to offer my warm congratulations and good wishes to your person, and to our country - hoping for both good fortune and prosperity.

As I was following your press conference of 7/7/1996, I was extremely worried by the accusations and threats to which my newspaper and myself were exposed. Thus I found no way but to write to you first, and to ask to meet you second.

Mr. President:
I am a citizen who is active in society using legal means and for constitutional objectives which I see and believe serve my country. My activities are not based on any group affiliation, political party, or local or foreign entities. I depend primarily on the will of God, and on the stipulations of the law and constitution in the country.

In my activities, I have worked to support the good efforts of society in the battle against corruption, carelessness and oppression.

Mr. President:
I contend that I am a decent and honest man who spends long hours at work. I stand at no one's doors asking for personal benefits - whether that person is a Yemeni or a foreigner. I have never received one Riyal or one dollar for me from any one (in return for illegal services as you contend). If you have been informed otherwise, Mr. President, I urge you to please refer the matter to the courts for my trial.

Mr. President:
My newspaper and I do not need you as an enemy. We need you as a friend (supporter).

I pray to God to guide you to the right path, one that serves our nation; and I wish you good health.

May God's peace, mercy and blessings be upon you.

Dr. Abdulaziz Al-Saqqaf
10/7/1996.

Unquote.

Yemen Times
Post Office Box: 2579
Sanaa, Republic of Yemen
Telephone +967 (1) 268 661/2
Facsimile # +967 (1) 268 663
Aden office : Phone/Fax 345 653

يمن تايمز: الحائزة على جائزة حرية الصحافة الدولية ١٩٩٥
Yemen Times: Winner of the 1995 International Press Freedom Award

فخامة الرئيس علي عبدالله صالح - رئيس الجمهورية المحترم

تحية طيبة وبعد :

أنتهز حلول ذكرى السابع من يوليو وقرب حلول ذكرى السابع عشر من يوليو ، لأتقدم إليكم بأحر التهاني وأطيب التبريكات متمنياً لشخصكم الكريم ، وللوطن الخير والإزدهار .

عند متابعتي للمؤتمر الصحفي الذي عقدتموه يوم ١٩٩٦/٧/٧ ، إنتابني قلقٌ شديدٌ من الإتهامات والتهديدات المباشرة التي تعرضتُ لها وصحيفتي ، ولم أجد بداً من الكتابة إليكم أولاً ، وطلب الإلتقاء بكم ثانية .

فخامة الرئيس :

إنني مواطنٌ ينشطُ في هذا المجتمع بالوسائل القانونية ولأهداف مشروعة فيما أرى وأعتقد أنه يخدم بلدي ، ولا أرتكز في ذلك على عصبية أو حزب ، أو أي جهة محلية أو خارجية ، بل أركن في ذلك أساساً على مشيئة الله ، ثم على سيادة النظام والقانون .

وفيما أنشط ، أسعى لرفد جهود مجتمعنا الخيرة في معركتنا ضد الفساد والإنفلات والظلم .

ياسيادة الرئيس :

أدعي أنني رجل شريف عفيف أقضي كل وقتي في العمل الدؤوب ، ولا أتسول أمام باب أي شخص - يمنياً أو أجنبياً. ولم يسبق أن إستلمت ريالاً واحداً أو دولاراً واحداً من أي جهة كانت . وإن بلغكم خلاف هذا ياسيادة الرئيس ، أطلب منكم الإحالة إلى القضاء لمحاكمتي .

إنني وصحيفتي لا نحتاج إلى خصومتكم ، ولكننا نحتاج إلى رعايتكم .

أدعو الله أن يأخذ بيدكم لما يحب ويرضاه ، ولما يخدم هذا الوطن ، وأتمنى لكم الصحة والعافية .

والسلام عليكم ورحمة الله وبركاته .

د/ عبدالعزيز السقاف
١٩٩٦/٧/١٠

Chapter 14: Reconciling with Saleh

I met President Saleh several times after that. I would usually get a call asking me to go to the Presidential palace, sometimes in the afternoon or evening, and join the President along with a number of officials, bureaucrats, tribesmen, and other members of Yemeni elites. I even once took my youngest, Raidan, with me to see the President, an experience he wouldn't forget. I was told that President Saleh liked to consult, and it was his way of keeping those he respected close, and make sure that he had access to them. We did not have a formal interview, not yet, but he was happy to answer any of my questions.

"Mr President, I note that most people who join you in these meetings are from the Zaydi stronghold regions. What about the rest of Yemen?" I asked him once.

"Ya Qubati, where are you from?" President Saleh shouted to a third person in response to my question.

"I'm from Lahj, ya Fandem," he responded.

"Ya Bouraji, where are you from?" he yelled to another person.

"I'm from Hodeida, Your Excellency, Mr President," he responded.

Then President Saleh looked at me and said, *"You see, I have some of these faggots around me,"* using the equivalent Arabic derogatory word with a look to say: what's your point?

YEMEN TIMES

• SANAA • January 20th thru 26th, 1997 • Vol. VII, Issue No. 3 • Price 30 Riyals

INSIDE:
- MP Abdullah Mahdi on Parliamentary Experience. Page 3.
- G. de Vita on Yemeni-Italian Relations. Page 5.
- Leprosy in Yemen: Visible Progress. Page 8
- Your lifestyle determines your longevity. Page 10.

Chatting at the Presidental Office: (from left) Vice President Abdo Rabbo Mansoor Hadi, YT Chief Editor Abdulaziz Al-Saqqaf, President Ali Abdullah Saleh, Raydan Al-Saqqaf, and Prime Minister Abdulaziz Abulghani.

President Saleh Stresses Coming Electi...

"The hard day are behind us."

In a visibly optimistic mood, General Ali Abdullah Saleh, President of the Republic announced, "The hard days are behind us." He said the country was growing out of its pains and hardships at many levels.

In two extended private conversations with the chief editor of the Yemen Times, Dr. Abdulaziz Al-Saqqaf, the President gave summary assessments of recent achievements, and his views on the future.

"At the political level, we have healed most of the wounds, and the next elections represent a watershed in our evolution. They will mark the final cohesion of our people. These elections are critical for Yemen.

"At the economic level, the n... and corrective measures have to bear fruit. We expect 1997 the economic launch year.
"At the military level, we rebuilt the army, navy and airf... an all-time high capability.
"At the foreign relations lev... have finally overcome the afte... of the Gulf War and the civil ... 1994. We are expecting 19... witness new break-throughs relations with our neighbors. The President said he extends h... to all those who want to help Yemen for the 21st century. "N... is blacklisted. All are welco... join the construction effort."

A New Low for the Dollar Exchange Rate

The US dollar exchange rate of the Yemeni Riyal hit a new low in the market this week. In yet the lowest exchange rate in a year, the dollar was selling at YR 124 in the open exchange market yesterday. For several months, the dollar exchange rate hovered around YR 128-130. This week, the Riyal gained a solid 5%. Experts believe that the exchange rate could witness another dip.

"There are many reasons for these developments. There is the optimism created by a more balanced government budget. There is the looming gas deal. In Ramadhan, many immigrants send home remittances. Most consumer goods were stocked earlier, thus tapering off demand for imports," explained Ahmed Thabit, Deputy General Manager of IBY.

Prime Minister Paints a Positive Picture:

"Economy is in an upswing."

Prime Minister Abdulaziz Abdulghani stressed that the Yemeni economy was in an upswing. Speaking in a press conference held at his office on Sunday, January 19th, the Prime Minister elaborated the many corrective measures taken and the various indicators that signal an improving economic situation in 1996. "1997 will be an even better year," Mr. Abdulghani said.

More on page 7

Lawyers, Feminists, Modernists to Fight New Personal Status Law Draft

A lobby bloc is taking shape. This brings together a number of lawyers, feminists, journalists, university professors, and many other modernists and human rights activists in order to fight the 145 changes the Lajnat Taqneen Ahkam Al-Shariyah Al-Islamiyyah (Committee to Enact Laws based on Islamic Sharia) wants to introduce in the present Personal Status Law (Qanoon Al-Ahwal Al-Shakhsiyyah).

"We are not against Islamic Sharia. To the contrary, we are demanding a full and correct implementation of the Sharia. But we are against the whimsical application of the Sharia based on the bias and twisted ideas of some individuals," said Shada Mohammed Nasser, a leading person in this bloc.

Ms. Amatul-Aleem Al-Sousuwah, Deputy Minister of Information and Chairman of the National Women's Group, indicated that she will campaign within the executive branch of authority against the new changes.

A group of activists are getting together next week to discuss the next step. "We shall chart out action plans for the period immediately following Eid Al-Fitr," Shada said.

Dunlop's World-famous Tyres
DRIVING TO THE FUTURE
HIGHEST QUALITY • FASTEST DELIVERY • BEST SERVIC

ZAMIL STEEL
The Largest Manufacturer of Pre-Engineered Steel Buildings in Asia

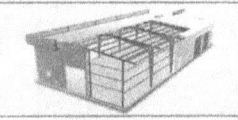

OVER 20,000 BUILDINGS SOLD SINCE 197...
FACTORIES
WAREHOUSES
SPORTS HALLS
AIRCRAFT HANGARS
SUPERMARKETS
ALMOST any ONE, TWO or THREE STOREY BUILDING

Mr. Ali Al Hussain, Resident Sales Executive
• Phone 23-6635, 23-6636 • Fax 23-5901

HIGHEST QUALITY • FASTEST DELIVERY • BEST SERVIC

I got to know President Saleh, and those around him, further in 1996 onwards, which gave me a closer insight into how the man thought. His governance style was akin to running through repeated crises in perpetuity, and he had to find a way to keep people on their toes. He was known to drive around town in his own car, but he increasingly started to make unannounced field visits across the country. I asked him once, "*Mr President, how many among the people around you actually help you do your job?*" And his reply was "*None,*" and that they were, in fact, a burden. President Saleh knew he was often surrounded by parasite-like officials who saw him as an opportunity for personal enrichment without contributing to his regime, and the longer they continued in positions of power, the worse his governance would be.

"*Mr President, how many people do you have in jail?*" I once asked him.

"*The ones I know of are around 10 or 12 thousand,*" he replied.

So I naturally asked, "*And the ones you don't know of?*"

He looked at me and said: "*You asked me about the things I don't know. How about you go find out and tell me?*" And then he added, "*We have no secrets.*"

Later that week in late 1996, I found my name among a few others who had been appointed as members of the newly established Consultative Council, which worked like a Senate. I wasn't asked or consulted. I actually had issues with the point behind that Consultative Council, used to "shelve" officials who underperformed or were found redundant, or other senior officials the President wanted to keep around on the payroll without alienating them. Aziza was happy with that appointment, which looked like a promotion. *Maybe now we'll move out from our apartment to a decent house*, she thought.

"*I'm not going to take it,*" I told Aziza.

"*Why not?*" she asked

"*It's a bribe, to silence me ahead of the next election,*" I replied.

"*Nothing wrong with being silent. Save us the trouble of spending too much and losing again in the next election,*" she said, rolling her eyes. She's already been through a lot of emotional trauma thanks to my adventures and misadventures.

"*Didn't you have enough? Maybe the next time they will take you away to never come back.*" She added, "*Now you have a chance to do something.*"

She was right. I had been offered senior government roles before, often in exchange for my silence or to soften my position on my principles. But this time, there was no such stipulation. I was given a job without any preconditions. In fact, the President had asked me last week to go find out how many people there were in jail that he didn't know about.

"*If I take the job, I won't take any money or rewards,*" I told Aziza.

The job of being a member of the Consultative Council was what you made of it. Upon my arrival, I started inquiring about how the council worked, what was on its docket, and how it engaged with other parts of government. At the time, the council had two tasks from the President: the first was coming up with a way to address blood feuds between the tribes, and the second was on how to improve efficiencies of the civil service. Being an academic, I proposed a methodology for studying both matters, tasking a group among its membership to take a closer look at the issue, consult with all relevant parties, and propose a course of action. The council was a clean slate with little that limited what it could do. This is something I could take advantage of to advance the human rights agenda, especially during this post-war era.

I also needed a team, my council position entitled me to hire two guards, an assistant, and an office manager. I didn't need the guards, so I hired two cadets whom I interviewed; one of them became a promising journalist, while the other continued in a civil service career. My office manager was *Yemen Times*'s own sports editor, Jamal Al-Awadhi. I picked him because he was savvy and had potential. More importantly, I needed a network of allies, particularly inside the council, to engage them in this work and have them adopt it as well.

Belonging to the World

Airing out the political tensions following the civil war allowed the second tier of issues to become paramount, particularly organized militias, terrorism, tribal conflict, and kidnappings. These were all issues for the post-war government, consisting mainly of GPC and Islah with tokenistic ex-YSP and southern figures. The cabinet itself was led by a long-time acquaintance of mine, Abdulaziz Abdulghani, who I first met in the US Embassy in 1975 during the Fulbright orientation. He was a fellow economist by training and a capable official, and he engineered many of the badly needed economic reforms the country required to accelerate toward socioeconomic wellbeing.

Going international would help cement Yemen's image as an emerging democracy, and thereby make it difficult to reverse our hard-won democratization, pluralism, and human rights gains. I had done extensive outreach to partners and friends in the international community to pay more attention and give our democratization more visibility. One positive response came through UNESCO, where we organized a regional seminar on Promoting Independent and Pluralistic Arab Media, held in January 1996. This seminar was important as it recognized that Yemen had something to offer at a regional level on this front.

This seminar was a big deal and we inflated it further. It was opened by Prime Minister Abdulaziz Abdulghani, six Ministers, representatives from the United Nations and the diplomatic community, and some 140 journalists from across the region and Yemen. The event produced the 1996 Sana'a Declaration that was adopted by UNESCO in 1997, and it had strong language supporting press freedom across the region. It also allowed visiting journalists to take note of Yemen's progress and keep an eye on it.

We also used that opportunity to seek training fellowships for Yemeni journalists abroad and organize training and coaching sessions in the country. Yemen Times hosted many such trainings, and some were organized in partnership with other institutions. We trained many promising young women and men who became our greatest assets as Yemen Times and also as a Country. Hatem Bamehriz is politically savvy, Nadwa Al-Dawsari is a force of nature, and Mohamed Al-Qadhi has an inquisitive spirit that knows no bounds. With such talents we continue to raise the bar for journalism in Yemen, nudging the country toward more sophisticated and capable journalism away from the partisan-charged reporting of the period before the war. Several investigative journalism articles were no less than award winning, revealing cases of corruptions, misconduct, abuse, and outright appropriation of public assets.

One story was about how a senior official took over a children's school in Hadhramout governorate, saying that he owned the land (due to a clerical error), and therefore the school – which he would now sell to the government or turn into a flea market. This story created a running joke where the offer was: Buy the school, get the pupils for free. Another story covered a known arms dealer importing a variety of firearms that were recorded at customs as automotive spare parts and taxed accordingly. The story was revealed thanks to an investigative journalist who uncovered the story trying to find an explanation for the reportedly high volume of "spare parts" imported from Eastern Europe and Russia.

I also had a few media engagements during this time on Yemen's democratization, including regional and global media. *Yemen Times* also coordinated a special sponsored section published in *Newsweek* entitled: "Yemen: Poised for Growth into the Next Millennium." That section included many topics about different commercial establishments like Yemenia Airlines, TeleYemen, Aden Free Zone Development Project, Hayel Saeed Anam Group of Companies, commercial banks in Yemen, tourist agencies, and many others. We were making progress and getting the world's attention. But we still had a lot of mending to do at home, including some genuine reconciliation following the 1994 civil war.

Yemen Times also started publishing summaries of international reports that discussed the situation in Yemen, such as reports by the United Nations, the US Department of State, Amnesty International, and others. It was important for Yemeni elite to see that the world was talking about us, and also to ensure that the Ministry of Information and the Political Security Offices knew this as well, through their respective translations of *Yemen Times*.

Chapter 15: Elections, Round 2

Yemen's next parliamentary elections were planned for April 1997. I seriously considered running again but wasn't sure. It felt like I was living a contradictory life, part of me living in the past recounting my failed run four years ago and what a second failure would do to me and my reputation, and part of me living in the future imagining a successful campaign and a new opportunity to contribute to Yemen's democratic development. Aziza said that if I ran again I would easily win, having established a good legacy through the Hadharem Welfare Association, and my recent appearance on Al-Jazeera. It was a timely interview in January 1997, on the 'Opposite Direction' talk show hosted by Faisal Al-Qassim, where I and Dr Ayed AlMane of Kuwait debated regional integration and the prospects of Yemen's accession to the Gulf Cooperation Council. That interview was rebroadcast in Yemen's national TV and sort-of gave me celebrity status.

My personal ambition aside, I felt perhaps I should take a closer look at what Yemen's democratization process needed. One line from my Al-Jazeera interview was that successful societies should look toward the future, and so it came to me. I had examined the experiences of other emerging democracies as they advanced on their respective journeys, and considered what guardrails they had in place that we could use in Yemen. Perhaps there was something else that I could do to support other candidates running in this election, protect the process's integrity, and ensure that the election strengthened Yemen's democracy.

Western Diplomats Express Support for EMC:
Ambassadors Briefed by EMC

he invitation of Ms. Shadha Mohammed er, Assistant Secretary-General for Technical rs of the Elections Monitoring Committee, ral ambassadors visited the EMC head office week.
Tuesday, December 3rd, the Ambassador of United Kingdom, the Honorable Douglas ton, and the Deputy Chief of Mission, Mr. d Pearce, visited the organization. The sh diplomats were received by Dr. Abdulaziz aqqaf, Secretary-General, Ms. Nasser. Mr. in Abdul-Razzaq, Director of the Legal artment, Dr. Mohammed Al-Maitami and y lawyers working for the EMC.
Thursday, December 5th, Mr. Giovanni de s, Deputy Chief of Mission at the Italian assy, visited. He was received by Dr. Abdu-Al-Saqqaf, Ms. Shadha Mohammed Nasser, Salwa Ahmed Qassim Dammaj, Assistant etary-General for Financial Affairs, and Mr. ed Al-Soufi, Director of Internal Volunteer ilization Department and other officials.
Saturday, December 7th, the Ambassador of United States of America, the Honorable id Newton, accompanied by Ms. Margaret ey, DCM, Mr. Adam Ereli, Information & ural Attache and Director of USIS, and ard Jarvis, Political Attache, visited. They e received by Mr. Mohammed Al-Rubayi,

Chairman of the EMC, Dr. Abduluziz Al-Saqqaf, Ms. Shadh Mohamed Nasser, and Yassin Abdul-Razzaq, Director of the Legal Department.
On Monday, December 9th, the Ambassador of the Kingdom of the Netherlands, the Honorable Arend Meerbrug, visited the EMC. He was received by Dr. Abdulaziz Al-Saqqaf, Ms. Shadha Mohammed Nasser, Dr. Ahmed Abdul-Qader, Director of the Foreign Relations Department, and several other officials.
The visiting diplomats were briefed on the work of the EMC and its various branch offices, the report on the Registration Phase of the Elections Process, and the plan of action for the future.
There were many questions about how the work was going and the positive contribution of the EMC to the elections process and the democratization effort. All diplomats, without exception,

expressed support for the work of the organization and indicated interest in continued contact and exchange of information.
Yemen Times learned that other ambassadors are planning to visit the EMC and share views with its executive board - all members of whom are working on a free and voluntary basis.
At another level, a consultant delegation representing the European Union is expected to arrive in Yemen this week. This delegation will hold talks with the Supreme Elections Committee, the Elections Monitoring Committee, and other relevant organizations. The purpose of the talks is to finalize arrangements for ways to channel EU support for these bodies.

By: Anwar Al-Sayyadi,
Yemen Times.

Following rounds of consultations, I decided that we could set up an apparatus that would monitor the elections, to ensure its integrity and validity, dubbed the Election Monitoring Committee (EMC). The recently approved electoral law empowered the Supreme Electoral Committee to run free and fair elections, and included provisions that organized the role of independent electoral monitors. The EMC was launched with support from the United Nations, NDI, Arab Organization for Human Rights, Ford Foundation, and other partners. Such a mission wasn't particularly expensive, but it was rather demanding from an organizational point of view.

This was a critical time in Yemen's history, as the YSP had boycotted the election and there were emerging rifts between the GPC and Islah. Furthermore, it looked like the GPC had entered a new era where it seemed more interested in dominating the political landscape and reducing the political space for dissenting or contrary views, including those of its allies. At one point, language from the 1980s single-party rulebook started to come back, especially as the GPC continued to use the public treasury as its own party purse and the State's assets for their own partisan purposes. Keeping a close eye on irregularities and whistleblowing was now more critical than ever.

The starting point was to spread the word among civil society, media, and other independent entities about this proposal, soliciting their interest in forming a committee to design an independent electoral observation mission and what they could bring to the table. I wanted to focus on the training and reporting modalities, so that national monitors knew what to expect, what was in line with the law and practice and what wasn't, and how to report on any irregularities. It was key to identify both blatant issues as well as subtle irregularities. The initial plan was to deploy just over 3,000 monitors, with roughly 10 per electoral district, and we designed a budget and a workplan accordingly.

The EMC's first report cited over 100,000 challenges and contestations in the registration stage of the elections alone. Islah filed 39% of those challenges, followed by the GPC with 32%. It was a six-month undertaking, all in all, and we had the base of operations at the ground floor of *Yemen Times*'s new premises, and established satellite offices in Taiz, Aden, Redaa, Hajjah, and Mukalla, hosted by partner NGOs in these locations. Thereafter we opened the door for expressions of interest for would-be monitors, organizing the training, and working with oversight and support structures to ensure the reliability of our own process. We also engaged with the Supreme Elections Committee, candidates, political parties, local authorities, and other stakeholders to sensitize them on our role and solicit their cooperation. It was heartwarming to see there was popular interest in running a successful election, particularly the vested interest by the GPC as the ruling party to ensure that the elections took place on time and without incident.

We also used the Internet to upload daily reports, briefs, instructions, and irregularity reports, among other information. It helped to manage a large process that required a heavy presence all over the country. This was a fantastic learning experience and taught us more about the divide between Sana'a and everywhere else in the country, which indicated the significant work needed to bridge this divide as we looked forward to a more decentralized governance structure and decision-making. Noting the patterns of participation, transparency, and cooperation in the various regions would help future rooting of Yemen's own future local democratic development.

It surprised me to realize that monitors from less-developed governorates like Amran and Mareb were keener to participate and more diligent in their work than their counterparts in more prosperous places like Taiz and Hadhramout. Their reporting was better, quicker, and more detailed. Perhaps it was their desire for a government that responded to their needs, seeing no viable recourse apart from working with the system and moving toward their future. Taiz colleagues for instance, although more educated, were more skeptical of the process. Possibly their communities received support from non-government actors that addressed their development challenges, such as remittances and philanthropy, and perhaps that's why they seemed less invested in a more responsive government.

With that thought, I felt Yemen would be alright: once the system started delivering for those who most needed it to deliver, the country would be able to move forward. The election was a straightforward exercise, with good organization and few grave incidents. The results also demonstrated how the GPC capitalized on the war and the strong pro-Unification propaganda, utilizing the

State's capabilities including media, civilian and non-civilian manpower, and resources to support its candidates. Furthermore, President Saleh's non-dogmatic and flexible leadership made the GPC home to almost anyone who mattered. The GPC ended up with 187 out of 301 parliamentary seats, with another 39 parliamentarians who ran as independents and later joined the GPC, akin to what happened in 1993.

The GPC therefore ended up with a comfortable majority of 75% to form the government and take the country forward, with a weaker opposition and seemingly shrinking space for dissent and contrary opinions. The Unified Yemen of 1990, which resulted from the agreement between the GPC and YSP, is now the Unified Yemen of 1997, where the GPC called all the shots.

Chapter 16: Making Progress

Despite the ups and downs, this country was making progress. Yemen was receiving more and more global attention, dignitaries and international officials were coming and going, and Yemen's connections in the world were increasing. An upswing in investors was promising for the economy, and economic reforms implemented to stabilize the economy were starting to show promise. A few development programs were bearing fruit, such as the work of the Social Fund for Development. I was also deeply encouraged by the talents of young Yemenis having had the opportunity to apprise the selection process of several scholarship programs for high achievers to study in Canada, the USA, Germany, and other advanced countries. I sincerely felt that tomorrow's leaders were around the country and would be able to leapfrog the country forward: Yemen's future was in good hands with these bright minds getting the helm.

To me, Yemen was like an infant child as it started to learn to walk. We take a few baby steps, fall, get hurt, cry a bit, but then we wipe our tears and get up to take a few more steps. Yemen did not have a hand to hold or a walker to help it take its first few steps without falling over and getting hurt, but we pulled through, and would continue to pull through. Yemen would learn to walk, march, run, and even dance. I believed in this country, and I knew we'd make it through.

And *Yemen Times* would run and dance too; it would be Yemen's dance partner.

Yemen Times Online

Nothing speaks progress like access to the latest technology. The year 1996 represented the dawn of the Internet in Yemen, and a most exciting opportunity for *Yemen Times* to establish its online presence and expand its global reach. Luckily, we had our very own software developer, my son Walid, who brought his ideas and creative genius to our online presence. *Yemen Times*'s first website had opened new avenues for interaction with a global audience, connecting with Yemenis abroad, undertaking online polls, and soliciting views and opinions from around the world. It was also the world's window into Yemen, significantly contributing to what the world knew about Yemen and how it could engage with it.

"*Coverage in the West of the Yemen human rights situation is sensational and one-sided*," said a diplomat who was collecting information on possible human rights projects to be financed by the European Commission in Yemen, so we needed Yemeni voices that spoke for Yemen with first-hand authority and experience. This doubled the responsibility of *Yemen Times* to show the progress Yemen was making, not just in the context of its history since unification, but also in contrast to the human rights situation across the region. There remained a lot more about Yemen that could and should be reported; we had an image problem, noting recent security incidents of kidnapping tourists, tribal conflicts, and underdevelopment.

By November 1997, *Yemen Times*'s website achieved over 1,000 hits a week, a significant expansion from the eight visits per day when it first started a year ago. Many of these visits originated from the USA and Europe, with a significant increase of readership referring to *Yemen Times*'s web address in various professional, diplomatic, and Yemeni expatriate networks. The website had become a significant tool in making Yemen a good world citizen by strengthening its connections to the world. Thank you, dear Walid, for your initiative and dedication, you made me most proud. You will have a great future ahead of you and will continue to do great things.

Particularly endearing is the link *Yemen Times* was able to make with Yemenis abroad, and how they used our website to connect with us, with each other, and with the country as a whole. We often got messages from Yemeni expatriates inquiring how they could help the country and asking us to connect them with various partners in support of Yemen. These supports ranged from donating books to libraries to organizing field hospitals staffed by visiting medical teams. I was particularly happy with how our website was linking Yemen to the world, and bringing the world to Yemen.

My Quadra 700

A year into the life of *Yemen Times*, we were able to piece together a shoestring but viable economic model using two Apple computers and minimum infrastructure. Our income relied predominantly on advertising that catered to the *Yemen Times* audiences, mainly in the travel, tourism, and hospitality sectors. We also had the occasional vacancy or other announcement, which were a welcome source of revenue and helped us reach a somewhat sustainable cashflow. It is true that the GPC did not look kindly at *Yemen Times* and discouraged the business community from advertising with us, but the newspaper had its loyal readership that also represented those with buying power in the country. I was happy to note that many in the business community in Yemen believed in *Yemen Times* and its mission and I'd built good friendships with many of them, including Alwan Al-Shaibani, Nabil Hayel, and Jamal Al-Mutarreb. To them and others, thank you for your support over the years.

The stable cashflow allowed us not only to expand the team but also upgrade our equipment. We brought in three more Apple computers, the Power Macintosh 4400/200s, and then we added a Quadra 700 and Quadra 840 Macintosh machines. That Quadra 700 was my trusty partner for a few more years, welcoming me with its characteristic Apple startup chime as it fired up to get the work done. It was almost saying *Let's get crackin. What stories do you have for me today, Abdulaziz!* These machines were our treasure in *Yemen Times*, and we would go to great lengths to ensure that they were functioning well and were protected from saboteurs. It was key for us to upgrade our technology when we could as it opened new horizons for us, not only in word processing and layout, but also in a design language that allowed *Yemen Times* to attract more advertising and readership.

Yemen Times also opened branches in Aden and Taiz, and we had stringers in six other cities as well. We also piloted printing simultaneous copies of *Yemen Times* in London and New York, but only for a short period before the costs racked up and we aborted this venture. Luckily, the Internet provided us with a more viable option to reach an international audience. This also helped us circumvent censorship and being denied use of the postal service to send *Yemen Times* to our international subscribers.

The biggest challenge was in printing *Yemen Times*. We outsourced that function to commercial printing establishments, which were also sometimes reluctant to print *Yemen Times* for fear of being shut down by the authorities. We also had issues with print quality, timelines of production, and continuously having to negotiate costs down. At one point, we were cornered to print only at the printing press of the armed forces guidance unit, who usually sent out an eye to read through the headlines before releasing the newspaper. Having to occasionally engage in hostage negotiations with your censor isn't a pleasant experience, and I remained adamant that *Yemen Times* had to get its own printing press.

Although we've upgraded since the Quadra 700 days with more modern machines, it remains in use with the multi-talented Ramzy in the office making use of it in the production cycle. I am comforted to know that my hardworking Quadra 700 is still there, should I need it.

Global Nomads in the Land of Sheba

Yemen Times has become a landmark stopover for foreign dignitaries, expatriates, and curious souls who come to Yemen to teach, learn, and experience something different. I've learnt a great deal from our guests; they were not only a connection to worlds beyond, but they contributed first-hand to the growth of *Yemen Times* and our team. We were always in need of professional journalists, editors, and proofreaders, and I capitalized on as many as possible. I recall asking a dear friend, Jenny Jobbins, to organize some of the first intensive training on journalism for *Yemen Times* staff, especially as we continued to have significant staff turnover. We couldn't pay much, yet we demanded a lot with tight and often stressful publishing deadlines. Plus, the opening of Yemen meant the influx of international organizations on the hunt for local talent, and *Yemen Times* was a talent factory graduating many outstanding and capable young women and men. We tried to do the same on the French side with Jerome Bernard leading that work, but that was an insurmountable task that eventually led to the discontinuation of the French pages in *Yemen Times*. It just never got enough traction, and I was happy that Saba News Agency had started a French Bulletin following their English one, so perhaps my job there was done, too.

One of the key concerns we had was the security of our expatriate staff. While most of them had other teaching, work, and life commitments that brought them into Yemen in the first place, I was worried that wearing the journalist hat would also create an additional bull's-eye on their back. Martin Dansky asked me once what to do in case he was kidnapped. I told him to mention he's Canadian, because everybody, including kidnapper tribesmen, love Canada.

I would be remiss not to mention my good friends Dr Riad Al-Khoury and Dr Ramakanta Sahu. Both were regular contributors, but I particularly appreciated Dr Sahu's focus on using *Yemen Times* to help young readers improve their English language skills, which resonated with me as a fellow educator. Over the years we had tens of other collaborators from across the world who made important contributions to *Yemen Times*: to them all our gratitude and most heartfelt appreciation.

We were a world community, working together through *Yemen Times* to make our beloved Yemen a good world citizen. But we did have our differences. Yemen tended to be seen more favorably by expatriates, perhaps because they had seen worse elsewhere in the world, or due to the region's own regressive politics and limited space for expression. I often took issue with that, as I was not interested in how bad things were or could be, I was interested in the bankable potential that Yemen could be. The dynamism of our transition could yield so much, and I needed people to help Yemenis see that. The benchmark shouldn't be a neighboring petrostate where the leaders were God-like figures; the benchmark was realizing our collective aspirations in a liberal democracy with a vibrant free market economy that worked for the benefit of Yemenis, peoples of the region and across the world.

Send in the clowns!

Yemen Times's headlines continued both to be critical and to uncover news that the government did not want reported. Despite the best of intentions, old tricks came to resurface again. A press officer at the Presidential palace established his own newspaper with funding from Saleh, called *Yemen Observer*, and it was designed to be a copycat of *Yemen Times* but of much inferior quality. It looked like a replica in terms of logo, format, structure, and even poached some of our own staff. Imitation is a form of flattery, and it was interesting to follow the *Yemen Observer*, and see how it translated Arabic-language official media, and reported on the issues *Yemen Times* raised but differently. I had actually called its editor and invited him over to *Yemen Times*, promoting the ideals of press freedom and the responsibilities associated with being a pressman.

"*Find your own voice and perspective*," I repeatedly told him. "*Your arguments need to respect the reader and say something meaningful, as this will give you more credibility*," I added. "*It doesn't matter where you started and who is bankrolling you, what matters is our collective responsibilities toward our citizens.*" I kept hammering at him, hoping for an improvement. I eventually gave him his space, hoping that the hard work that went into putting together a newspaper would help him achieve the maturity needed for our line of work. Unfortunately, my advice didn't resonate with him, so we published this occasional disclaimer to the *Yemen Times*'s readership above the cover page headline in bold font: "*Next time you buy your copy of Yemen Times, make sure you get the real paper, not the clown's copy, we mean, the clone copy!*"

All in all, the world's attention to Yemen and human rights in Yemen was paying off. Now almost all Yemeni officials and policymakers said that they believed in the virtue of human rights and insisted that they said so based on their own volition and values. There have been visible improvements in the human rights record in Yemen despite the glaring violations. However, most of their violations were due to ignorance and the autocratic culture rather than 80s-style premeditated political violence. Due process was slow, cumbersome, backlogged, and stretched, but it was there, and it was sort-of working, and improving at that.

But those improvements were plateauing. We'd come a long way since the 1970s and 80s, and we were seeing many of the critical cases being blocked for one reason or another. President Saleh's long-standing strategy of dealing with habitual human rights abusers was by sidelining them, promoting them, or appointing them next to me in the Consultative Council. He'd also become more sensitive to geographic and regional representation in his appointments, especially from the South and non-tribal areas.

Notwithstanding this progress, more work was needed. On November 13, 1997, the British Parliament issued a statement indicating their disgruntlement with the status of human rights in Yemen, and that statement was issued while President Saleh was on an official State visit to the UK. He was jolted by the statement, and it looked like he was at the end of his lip-service rope, and needed to do more serious work.

Chapter 17: Human Rights at the Consultative Council

Reception to the work of the Consultative Council was largely positive, and the government was instructed to implement the recommendations. At this point, I drafted a proposal to establish a permanent Committee for Human Rights at the Consultative Council, which would work similarly to a parliamentary committee tasked to advance human rights. My proposal was approved, and I was appointed as Chair of Yemen's Consultative Council's Human Rights Committee.

Right. This move raised many eyebrows, and some of *Yemen Times*'s readers wrote to me saying that we had softened our stance and I had been co-opted. I agreed that it might seem that way, however it was necessary to tone down our language as we work toward something meaningful, especially given international partners were advocating loudly for meaningful steps in advancing human rights. In parallel, I orchestrated a plan with deputy Minister of Interior Rashid Jarhum to organize a field trip to select prisons in five southern governorates, where the strongmen President Saleh appointed there had imprisoned anyone and everyone they suspected of being sympathetic to the banished YSP leadership or their succession plans. These prisons were full, and they were causing significant frustration and disenfranchisement among the people of the South and human rights activists.

In November 1997, President Saleh undertook a "planned surprise" visit to the prisons Jarhum and I had visited to free thousands of prisoners. He sent clear messages to the political leadership and security apparatus indicating that such illegitimate detainment of civilians would no longer be tolerated. I used this messaging to arrange the release of over 2,000 prisoners from Sana'a, Hajjah, Hodeida, Taiz, and Aden, in addition to some of the smaller jails in the secondary cities of those governorates. We'd reached a point where sending out a message of inquiry about prisoners to governors, corrections officials, district attorneys, and courts administrators was often enough to cause the release of some wrongfully detained persons. We also had a hotline established to handle cases for prisoners of conscience.

In January 1998, the Human Rights Committee at the Consultative Council issued a comprehensive report on the total number of prisoners in Yemen, which stood at around 85,000, with 6% of them foreigners. I sent a fifteen-page summary of the report to President Saleh with a cover note, saying here is the number, now you know.

Nonetheless, the work was far from over as egregious violations of human rights still occurred. One case was that of Dr Al-Muhatwari, where this pious man was dragged from his religious center on false and malicious accusations. It felt like the security apparatus informants had arrest quotas that they needed to fill and were becoming increasingly desperate to justify their continued 1980s-like existence. Dr Al-Muhatwari's case was one of many, and the patterns were increasingly visible to us as we investigated more.

It was bound to happen. On July 30, 1998, I tendered my resignation to President Saleh. Not only had the number of prisoners increased, but the newfound improvised measures to operationalize the Consultative Council were curbed. "*Mr President,*" I wrote in my resignation letter, "*you use the Consultative Council as dumping grounds for individuals you want to appease while paralyzing their actions,*" adding that I'd find other ways to serve my country outside the government.

President Saleh rejected my resignation for the time being, but I kept a draft handy should I need to re-submit it again as I drew plans for the council to celebrate Human Rights Day on Dec 10th in a big way. Those plans would include audacious demands for a government-funded campaign to promote human rights, including putting the text of the Universal Declaration on Human Rights and its explanation in layman terms into cassette tapes for the public, and asking law enforcement officers to swear adherence to it on that day's ceremonies. I was interested to see how much of this would materialize.

Overall, my work with the Consultative Council was helpful in elevating the respect for human rights and elevating the status of journalism as a protected role. Work in media requires strong faith in this profession, its purpose, and contributions to society, coupled with permanent dissatisfaction with the levels of transparency and accountability. This is why the press is often described as the fourth estate and its role was vital to Yemen's democratization. But just as we continued to push for more space to do our work, pushback and harassments became more persistent, violent, and even creative at times.

Yemen 21st Century Forum

The stagnating progress was causing me to worry about the future of my country. Literally, this was a daily worry. I looked at three, five, and ten years down the road, and I worried. Most of the key people who managed our affairs had been at it for the last thirty years or so. In fact, they were directly responsible for the mess we were in today. These men need to be changed. The structure of our administration needed to be changed. Our value system and incentives needed to be changed.

In June 1998, I co-organized the first General Conference of NGOs in Yemen. I'd had multiple issues with the Minister of Social Affairs, Al-Batani; he was an old man who headed the ruthless State Police (sort of KGB) in the former South Yemen. He was another "I am the law" character, and I had a brush with him back in 1995, when following *Yemen Times* coverage of the war he decided to first suspend the board of the Hadharem Welfare Association, and then to hand-pick a replacement board from GPC members – some of whom had never even heard about the association. He then ordered that the association's Women Development Center – which was founded through privately mobilized means in 1993 and 1994, be transferred to a different association altogether. When the local community refused, he sent armed officers to enforce that illegal decision. The officers sieged the village for three days and terrorized everyone; they even forcefully occupied my own home. We had to get an injunction to get them out, and went to court to protect our center.

After eight months of litigation, a landmark decision declared all the steps taken by the government to be null and void, stating that the actions taken by the government and their repercussions were not in the best interest of the people of the region. With a minister like that, who obviously didn't respect the law or understand the concept of civil society, it was difficult to imagine him nurturing civic engagement and democratic development. Subsequently, as the June conference concluded, civil society was a pillar of the Yemen we wanted to build, and we needed to find a new way to elevate the quality of civic engagement despite the Minister's efforts to undermine it.

Hence, the Yemen 21st Century Forum. Established in October 1998 as an NGO incubator and support facility, the Forum's mission was to build Yemen's civil society sector. The Forum functioned like an American-style think tank, where intelligent people gathered to devise plans and strategies. Our goal was to chart a plan for Yemen's development over the course of the next 100 years. The absence of long-term thinking in Yemen was endemic; in fact, when my good friend Dr Abu Baker Al-Qirbi was honored as *Yemen Times*'s person of the year for 1994, it was in recognition of his groundbreaking effort in putting together Yemen's first generational strategy for education during his tenure as Minister of Education. The Forum therefore had five objectives centered around two themes: logistical and operational support for promising civil society initiatives, and substantive advisory support on all matters relating to Yemen's future over the next century.

It was an audacious, different endeavor, and around two dozen thought leaders gathered in support of the Forum. These included me, Dr Faraj Bin Ghanim, Mr Faisal Bin Shamlan, Dr Abubakar Al-Qirby, Engineer Mohammed Al-Tayyeb, Mr Mohammed Abdo Saeed, Dr Waheeba Fare'e, Brigadier Yahya Al-Mutawakil, Mr Jarallah Omar, and Sheikh Yahya Al-Habbari, among many others. We had identified three flagship initiatives to focus on: namely, to map Yemen's civil society toward effective empowerment as a sector; to develop a modern evidence-base as a one-stop-shop for data and information about Yemen as a preamble to the Yemen Transparency Organization; and to publish an annual report dubbed Yemen's "State of the Nation." We also agreed on strategic opportunities to leapfrog this work, such as the 2001 local government elections and NGO capacity development for anti-corruption.

The Forum received financial and political support from Germany, the Netherlands, the UK, Japan, Canada, and of course *Yemen Times*. We received a multitude of queries from international organizations, other partners, and many civil society representatives. The Forum was creating the right kind of buzz, at least to some, as it also raised the level of concern among Saleh's inner circle who had much to lose through having over 3,000 NGOs working to expose corruption and mismanagement.

Chapter 18: Thieves Don't Build Nations

The problem with Yemeni politics was that it had become a get-rich-quick scheme, where those connected with President Saleh and the regime were able to amass more wealth and influence. Those around the President competed for unearned privilege that gave them a false sense of entitlement to the public treasury. They'd rather have a new Land Cruiser for their own use than have that same money provide drinking water for a few thousand people in Tehama. I wondered how they could sleep at night. This didn't only corrupt political life, but it also distorted our values as a society where the source of one's wealth should be one's work. President Saleh tolerated the thieves and crooks around him because he had accepted it as a price to be paid to appease strong power centers. The monsters he created had grown out of control, and increasingly prioritized their own personal enrichment even at the expense of Saleh's own regime.

Back in Sana'a University, I worked with students to go to the central bank and various ministries to take a closer look at government accounts and public finances. Some of my students' observations stayed with me for a while. I knew that our public accounting was never up to the standard, but some of the questions they raised needed further investigation. It took just over a year to gather the needed information, but we did.

On November 9, 1998, *Yemen Times* published a headline entitled "$22,500,000,000" as the dollar inflow into government coffers over the last twenty years. The article showed the volume of oil produced by Yemen, as well as the foreign assistance the country had received.

The paper asked for explanations how the money was used. The point of that article was to highlight what was already on everyone's minds, and provided a numerical figure to put it in context.

YEMEN TIMES

• SANAA • November 9th thru 15th, 1998 • Vol. VIII, Issue No. 45 • Price 30 Riyals

Dollar Inflow Over the Last 20 Years: WHERE DID IT GO?

$22,500,000,000

Not many people can readily read the above number?

It represents the total amount of hard currency the Yemeni authorities have received over the last twenty years. The US$ 22.5 billion or YR 3,260 billion, yields an average of nearly one and a half million riyals for every Yemeni family.

The main question Yemeni citizens ask is where did all that money go? Of course, some of the money was used for development projects. There is visible evidence to that all around. But a good part of the money was pocketed by crooked government officials and military/security officers working for the state. Also dipping into the bounty

Main Sources of Revenue to the State Over the last 20 Years in million US$

Cumulative Revenue from Oil	10,000
Saudi Arabia	2,400
The World Bank	1,160
Germany	720
Japan	586
The Netherlands	541
Un Bodies (UNDP, WFP, etc.)	453
Kuwait	362
International Monetary Fund	350
Abu Dhabi Development Fund	297
The European Union	246
Others	5,375
TOTAL	**22,500**

are tribal sheikhs and other civilians who are part of the entourage of our political leadership.

The largest source of dollar revenue to the state during this period has been the export of oil. Total Yemeni oil output, so far, is roughly one billion barrels. On average, if the Yemeni authorities' net income is US$ 10 per barrel, total revenue for the authorities from oil exports is roughly US$ 10 billion.

From the donors' side, the largest donor is Saudi Arabia. Though Saudi aid to Yemen stopped some nine years ago, it is still the largest, representing over 10% of the total inflow of hard currency to the country.

Today, the West (Germany, the Netherlands, Japan) as well as the UN bodies and multilateral donors (e.g., World Bank, EU, etc.) are the largest and most important donors to Yemen. Total annual revenues from Western bilateral and multilateral loans and grants nearly match the annual revenue of US$ 600 million the country gets from oil exports.

The issue of how the resources available to the Yemeni state is used is expected to be a major issue in the 1999 presidential elections, although it will not affect an already pre-determined result. But it will no doubt touch a few nerves here and there within the ruling oligarchy.

1,000,000,000 Barrels So Far

Last week, Yemen's total oil production topped one billion barrels. Since Yemen Hunt Oil Company started pumping in 1986, the company has produced until November 6th, some 660,000,000 barrels of oil. Canadian Occidental Petroleum Yemen has similarly produced another 322,000,000 barrels.

In terms of revenue, if the Yemeni Government netted an average of US$ 10 per barrel, which is a low estimate for the period until 1996, that means a total income of US$ 10,000,000,000.00.

While most Yemenis think the oil age has yet to dawn, oil production is falling.

Eritrean Leader Asks Yemen to Mediate in Ethio-Eritrean Dispute:

Yemeni-Eritrean Relations: A FRESH START

Eritrean President Asaias Afewerke completed a 3-day visit to Aden last week. He held several meetings with President Ali Abdullah Saleh and other officials on bilateral relations, and regional security and cooperation. "Differences and disputes exist among family members. The point is not to let such disputes get out of hand," the Eritrean President told the press.

He indicated the leaders of the 2 countries desired to overcome the Hanaish problem and re-launch stronger ties and cooperation. The Eritrean President also asked the Yemeni leader to use his good offices with Ethiopia in search of a negotiated settlement to the border dispute between the two African neighbors.

Yemen & Saudi Arabia: CHANGE OF HEART?

There has been a considerable growth of goodwill between the leaderships

The leaders of Yemen and Saudi Arabia exchanged key letters in two months. He

One Yemeni opposition politician found the warming up

Then all hell broke loose.

When *Yemen Times* printed the story, we felt we doing our job as watchdogs. We also believed that President Saleh was starting to become serious about introducing accountability into the system and control some of the monsters around him. We expected some heat, but not to the level that we endured. The harassment was unprecedented. I got a barrage of threatening phone calls from senior officials in the State. My personal car was smashed from two sides in a car 'accident'. The paper's premises were visited by security personnel. I was taken for interrogation by the Media Prosecutor. And the paper was attacked in the official media. It was the usual tactics but at an unprecedented intensity.

What was new were two articles, published by *26 September Newspaper* – the mouthpiece of the armed forces headed by the President's press secretary, and a similar one published by *Al-Mithaq* newspaper, the mouthpiece of the ruling GPC party. Both articles accused *Yemen Times* of serving foreign interests and publishing lies, and questioned my morals.

The *26 September Newspaper* also carried another article on page 2 on the same edition published on January 7, 1999. This article openly threatened me. First, it accused me of high treason, of conspiring against the supreme interests of the nation, and of working for Western intelligence agencies, international Zionism, and the masonic movement. But that was not all. The paper, in addition, ominously wrote: "*Saqqaf is working his way to suicide.*" Printing open threats in official newspapers against editors and journalists was not only contrary to President Saleh's messaging and official policy, but it was also a crime punishable by law. The President and his men knew very well that I had never worked against the interests of Yemen. Moreover, I did not see myself as an enemy of President Saleh or the regime. I criticized their mistakes, and would continue to do so, as that feel within my duty as a patriot and as a journalist. I served Yemen's interests by doing that.

The same edition of *26 September Newspaper* added a cartoon depiction on its last page portraying a belly dancer dancing on what looked like a pool of blood, saying: "*Clap for the Saqqaf, he wants to know where the money went? You don't get to. Understood, smarty-pants?*" The barrage continued for longer as well, so I had to take action to protect myself and my staff.

In a published letter, I decided to take this issue global and authorized the following four organizations to take the matter to court: The Committee to Protect Journalists in New York, Reporters Sans Frontiers in Paris, Federation of Arab Journalists in Cairo, and the Regional Office of the International Organization for Journalists. This was an unprecedented move in the Yemeni scene, and it seemed to have worked in slowing down the barrage of attacks. The Ministry of Information wanted to settle the matter in court two months after publication, and so to court we went, for the third time. The hearing on this case was scheduled for 2 June 1999.

Human Rights under Siege

The outcome of the 1997 elections gave the GPC a blank cheque to take the country forward, and it appeared that the GPC decided to rather nudge the country backward to the days of the 1980s authoritarianism through more repression and control. There were eight newspapers haunted by cases in court in early 1999, including *Yemen Times*. The others included *Al-Ayyam, Al-Haq, Al-Shoura, Al-Thawri, Al-Rai Al-Aam,* and *Ray,* among others. There were several journalists and columnists who are in prison.

On Saturday, February 6, 1999, Abdul-Latif Al-Kutbi, Chief Editor of *Al-Haq*, was released following a four-day ordeal in prison. Haitham Al-Ghareeb, lawyer and columnist, still languished in prison in Aden. Noman Kaied Saif, had been released from prison after three days in prison, not to mention suspension of his salary. Mohammed Al-Hadhiri's brother was mistakenly beat up in place of his journalist brother. *Al-Ayyam*'s chief editor was summoned for interrogation on what his paper had published, as was I on a separate case. Two newspapers – *Al-Shoura* and *Al-Rai Al-Aam* – were blocked from circulation. All of this happened in the span of less than a month.

Most of the harassment came from the Political Security Organization (PSO). Which did not have a clear mandate or even a law that regulated its work. I appealed to President Saleh flagging that the PSO needed to be brought within the law and must be regulated. I informed him that the intensity of violence and harassment against journalists was unprecedented, and how this would hurt his public image with the presidential elections planned for less than a year away. I was gravely worried about the trajectory this would pull the country toward, which would involve inflicting more suffering on the Yemeni people, and bring more instability to the nation.

At one point, about fifty or so pro-democracy activists came together to discuss the deterioration of the political climate, including some new faces, and I heard the following conversation in the background.

Person 1: "*You look familiar, don't I know you from somewhere?*"

Person 2: "*I don't know... I don't think so... Maybe at the meeting last month?*"

Person 1: "*What meeting?*"

Person 2: "*The Seminar at the University... maybe not...*"

Person 1 suddenly turned red and flushed with rage, and said: "*I remember you, you hit and tortured me at the PSO. I remember you and remember your ring. This ring you're wearing right now.*"

Then fighting ensued. The crowd was quick to intervene and let the PSO officer leave. We knew that the PSO was sending officers under cover to monitor us: we called them mosquitos. But I suppose there was only so many of them following all of us, so we were bound to cross paths again. Many colleagues had become even more paranoid about new entrants into journalism, asking about their work, publications, and for a literal reference check. Abdulbari Taher would ask, "*Do you have democracy in your blood?*" only to be interrupted by Ahmed Al-Haj who would laughingly say, "*Ask if they have blood first, then ask if they have democracy in their blood.*"

Yemen's political climate had soured tremendously over those months. It seemed sometimes that the clock was going back to the days of authoritarianism. Not if we could help it.

Taking a Look Back

By 1999 I was wearing six hats, first being father and family man; then professor of economics at Sana'a University; publisher and editor-n-chief of *Yemen Times*; chairman of Hadharem Welfare Association; Member of the Consultative Council and Chairman of its Human Rights Committee; and now Managing Director of the Yemen 21 Century Forum. Was this a lot to do? Probably, and I am sure I neglected many of my duties in the various roles, particularly toward my family and my students. But I take solace that my higher calling was to be in service of Yemen, all of Yemen, and – through Yemen – in service of the world.

Although a lot of progress was made, Yemen's transition hadn't reached the stage of being irreversible; it was like riding a bicycle where if you stop, you fall. This is why it was important to keep on pedaling and engaging positively in the democratization process until we completely removed the master-client relationship in Yemen's power structure, and replaced it with a political class answerable to the people.

Unfortunately, the President of the Republic had become enshrined as the patron-in-chief, where he was the source of wealth from the gifts and benefits he conferred on those connected to him. Many of those businesses were owned by his cronies and would have gone under had it not been for government contracts, and many of our senior officials would be unemployed given their lack of skills and capacity. So with these dependencies, they would do whatever was required to keep these benefits, even if it was dirty, illegal, immoral, and jeopardized the country's wellbeing and future.

The ultimate result of this was that Yemen would be held back and unable to make real progress. Viable businesses would go elsewhere, and efficient and capable people would leave or become marginalized. The overall mismanagement, nepotism, and corruption would cause an unforgivable disaster.

Averting this disaster is why we strove toward political democratization and economic transformation, aimed at creating a level playing field in which all players could compete on an equal footing. Accountability and transparency had to become standard tools to make all players, including top politicians, play by the rules. Those who could deliver and contribute would get ahead, and those who couldn't would be pushed aside.

After nearly a decade of trial and error in our country's evolution, I was starting to conclude that our President Saleh understood this, yet he made the decision to slowly abort Yemen's transition to the future it needed – the future I wanted for it.

Chapter 19: The Trial

It was almost 10 in the morning of June 2, 1999, and the court was in session. The fifty-year-old courtroom had never been this full. Something was in the air and everyone in the room knew this was no ordinary hearing. I could see several familiar faces all over the room.

My lawyer and long-time friend, Aallow, leaned toward me and said, "*Look how lucky you are, every intelligence agency has sent a high-level officer to attend your hearing. Even the Saudis sent their operator.*"

"*Hey*" I replied, "*the hearing hasn't even started yet and you are already causing trouble.*"

But he was right. I was scared and uncertain what would happen today. Truthfully, I had never expected this to come so far. If this issue was truly grave, then I would already be dead. But here I was, alive and well, and, in fact, I could do some socializing in this courtroom with these fine officers – pun intended – until the session started.

Just as I finished that thought, the bailer stood and cleared the desk for the judge, shuffling paperwork erratically. The prosecutor at the other end was looking through his notes and papers, and someone mumbled something in his ear to which he responded with a dismissive "*not now*" hand gesture. More people were flocking into the already-stuffed room; some seemed to know Aallow and waved hello. Some waved hello to each other as friends; others waved hello as adversaries. I was not sure what his plan was, but I trusted he knew what he was doing. We'd been through many ups and downs together, and he spent his life in court and knew how to pull things off, and how to wrestle with the law before yanking the eventual acquittal.

I'd run the scenarios for this day many times in my head. It couldn't really end well – and that was me being an optimist. How often did President Saleh want something and not get his way? I was just another name in a long list of journalists, politicians, and human rights activists who didn't sing his song, or maybe he wanted to make an example out of me because I was all three, sort of?

Today there were seven newspapers on trial in Yemen: *Al-Ayyam*, *Al-Ray-Aam*, *Al-Haq*, *Al-Shoura*, *Al-Thawri*, *Ray*, and *Yemen Times*. The charges varied, but it was always due to something the papers had printed. All cases were filed by the authorities. Five of us were on trial before Judge Al-Raimi in this court, being sued by the authorities for slander. *Al-Ayyam* was also on trial in Seera Primary Court in Aden for inciting separatist feelings, while *Al-Haq* was on trial in the North Sanaa Primary Court for printing what the press prosecutor termed "sensitive information," whatever that meant.

The authorities were tightening the screws on the media, even as the nation prepared to present itself as a model for democratization through the highly anticipated "Emerging Democracies Forum" to be held in Sana'a on the 27th of this month.

But this wasn't my first time in court. I was already detained seven times, albeit for short periods of time. I was beaten up twice. The paper was shut down once, and we'd been continuously subjected to various forms of harassment, including cutting off all communication lines, electric lines, tapping telephones, sabotage, censoring mail, intimidation, name calling, accusations ranging from national and high treason to being agents of the USA, Europe, Saudi Arabia, Kuwait, etc.... You name it.

The tension in the room escalated when the judge showed up on time. This was usual and they were often delayed in their quarters by "VIP visitors" who give them instructions or special packages, or they sometimes simply took their sweet time, a living representation of the saying "can't hurry justice," often said sarcastically when you needed to grease the wheels of the law. Justice can be yours if the price is right.

"All rise! The honorable Judge Al-Raimi presiding, in case number 311 for 1998, of the Ministry of Information against Yemen Times newspaper and Dr Abdulaziz Al-Saqqaf. Prosecutor Abdullah representing the claimant, Lawyer Aallow representing the defendant. We will now listen to opening arguments. Prosecutor Abdullah you have the floor."

Abdullah was a well-known and reputable prosecutor. He was known to be fair but harsh. His career was as old as this building, in fact I had met him once when investigating the story of the Aden-Abyan Islamic Army, a radical militia responsible for the execution of tourists just two years before. He told me, off the record, that there was no "green light" to proceed with legal action, and that insurgency should be handled as purely a security issue. This linked to the GPC's feelings of being shackled by some of its associates in Islah who were involved with the militia leaders. Therefore, an exposé might be politically damaging to both as the GPC steered Islah to creating "like-minded friends" all over the South. Anyway, Abdullah knew how the system worked and how to navigate the judicial system in a way that appeased the political leadership and allowed sensitive cases to find their way to a no-lose (not a win-win) resolution. Perhaps that's why he was named the prosecutor in my hearing.

"*Yemen Times, and Dr Abdulaziz, are both reputable media institutions in the service of Yemen...*"

Abdullah's opening line took me by surprise. It was not his usual language. In fact, it wasn't part of the legal practice to start with such a positive opinion. I was told that the President hired an international crisis management consultancy to deal with my case, but I dismissed that as rumors. Maybe you can teach an old dog new tricks. Abdullah continued:

"*They have contributed to the political development of Yemen in a positive and genuine way in many areas. Many of the stories that Yemen Times have published were always at the highest standards of professionalism and impartiality. However, in recent years, the quality of journalism in Yemen Times has started to decline, and the Ministry has concerns on the reliability of the analysis that can be misleading to public opinion. Our case here today is an example of that.*"

I thought I was starting to see what was going on here. I was asked prior to the trial to prove the numbers quoted in the article that caused this stir. This was *Yemen Times*'s headline asking where the $22.5 billion had gone. That demand was actually illegal because journalists are not required to divulge their sources. But I felt that Abdullah wanted documents to show how that number came about in order to steer the case, and I gave him proof in the form of documents that show the authorities had received more than US $27 billion. The number increased as I received some additional evidence from various sources after that article was published.

I believed Abdullah to be a fair and reasonable man. This same case was initially shelved for a few weeks after I gave him that information but then revived, probably due to political pressure. Now both of us needed to find a way to create an amicable resolution, especially with the milestone Emerging Democracies Forum later this month.

Despite our differences, President Saleh had shown some tolerance for democracy and I was positive we could figure out a way for this judicial process to proceed. In fact, this might be President Saleh's way of spinning the focus to demonstrate the maturity of political life in Yemen. This wasn't really a new trick, but an advanced stage of spin that President Saleh had mastered.

"On November 9th, 1998, Yemen Times published an article on its front page that referred to misappropriation of 22.5 billion dollars over the last twenty years, making unsubstantiated accusations of corruption and engaging in politically motivated misinformation," said Prosecutor Abdullah, adding: *"The Ministry of Information asked Yemen Times to retract this obviously misleading statement. Yemen is a State with established public financial management, and we have regular financial reports and audits, through which you can see that the amount is a significant exaggeration, is not based on realistic facts, and is distorted to sway public opinion. My office has gathered information on the claims made in that Yemen Times newspaper article, however it could not independently verify that information through the Ministry of Finance or the Central Organization for Audit, and therefore found no evidence of misappropriation or wrongdoing."*

Yeah... right... The thieves found no evidence of their crimes. They probably didn't hire a crisis management company but this was indeed an old-school spin situation to cover up the case. I appreciated Abdullah's attempt at professionalism, but to say he found no evidence of misappropriation was far from convincing. He was simply opening up the evidence to the court to examine, a process that would take forever. All the faces around knew the drill and we'd be adjourned until the court went through the evidence. But hey, it wasn't as if he could say anything different and get to keep his job, or possibly the head on his shoulders.

"Mistakes can happen. However, when the Ministry of Information asked Yemen Times to rectify the situation they refused, which is why we are asking for an official retraction, a two-year suspension of Yemen Times's license to operate, and a six-month suspended jail sentence for Dr A-lSaqqaf."

And with that, Abdullah concluded his statement.

I couldn't help but shake my head in disbelief. *That's all they ask?* I was not sure if they lowered the bar purposefully to avoid going to trial to complete the spin, at least in the eyes of the international community. Or maybe this was the carrot and there was a hefty stick awaiting me? I was not sure what to think. I was expecting a series of harsh accusations of treason, being an instrument for disturbing the political system, and what not. Something that I couldn't possibly, and under any circumstance, plead guilty to.

But before I could even gather my thoughts, It was Aallow's turn to speak. He nudged me gently, as if to say *"I got this."* If anyone knew the legal system and how to maneuver through it then it was Aallow, but this was no ordinary hearing, no ordinary case, and no ordinary day. I saw many attendees writing notes and dying to gossip with one another about what was going on. The room was awkwardly silent, even the usual troublemakers dying of suspense.

"Thank you, Your Honor. I'd like to echo the remarks of my colleague Abdullah, and agree that Yemen Times and Dr Abdulaziz are trying to contribute to making Yemen a better place for all of us and our children and grandchildren. And a human being is prone to making mistakes, only those who put in an effort are likely to make mistakes, and those who do nothing are the ones without mistakes..."

Where is this going? I thought to myself. *Does he want me to accept guilt and comply with the prosecutor's request?* Two years suspension would kill *Yemen Times* and damage the cases for the other newspapers as well. Furthermore, the suspended jail sentence would be proof of my guilt that could kill my reputation and damage my future work. But before I even finished that thought, Aallow surprised all of us by saying:

"This is why I think we should all look into the investigation that led to that article. I have here three boxes of documents that the defense would like to submit as additional evidence. These documents are the work of Yemen Times and a range of collaborators that showcase the basis for that article. A trial is the only fair way of showing if indeed the article is right, in which case Yemen Times will keep its license, but more importantly, it is the only way we can know the truth about the money."

The silent room went into a frenzy of gossip and awe. I can't begin to describe how skeptical crowd reacted to that statement, many of whom had their own conspiracy theories about how this trial had been pre-orchestrated with pre-determined results. Aallow was obviously looking for a fight with the headlines being three boxes of additional evidence, but calling out the prosecutor and the Ministry of Information like that was much more than a simple stunt. He knew we were not there to present evidence at this opening session, and the way he had his subordinates stand up carrying boxes of documents was more a dramatic show than a genuine attempt to submit evidence. In fact, the information I shared with him about the research leading to the article was less than one box!

"SILENCE... Silence..." the judge interrupted. *"This is a hearing to decide if this matter will go to trial, you cannot submit evidence here. Do you have anything else to add?"*

It was obvious that the judge didn't want to be there just then or preside over my case, especially not if he had to be dealing with the infamous Aallow. From the start, it seemed like the instructions given to Abdullah and the judge were not to go for a full trial but settle the matter there and then. If I pled guilty, I could negotiate the charges, and it would be a win for the Ministry and a good spin for President Saleh. But the problem for me was not only that it would hurt *Yemen Times* and the many staff and their families who depended on it, but it would set a precedent and reverse some of the gains freedom of the press had made in Yemen.

I didn't know what to think.

In my discussions with Aallow and his team, we worked out a scenario-based strategy. The first scenario was the heavy-handed usual practice, with accusations and what not, in which a trial was necessary to safeguard my reputation and keep *Yemen Times* open. The second was an under-the-table deal to slow things down, given Yemen's first Presidential elections planned in a few months' time. This scenario meant that the trial was a coercion tactic, but softening the editorial policy was definitely better than the alternative, which could cost me my life. And the third scenario was somewhere in between. But we haven't exactly planned for this.

"*Yes, Your Honor,*" Aallow replied. "*I have seven points that I would like to communicate in my statement, which I think are important for the court.*

"*Six years ago, the Ministry of Information sued Yemen Times for a different story, when the newspaper, allegedly, misquoted President Saleh, but we were acquitted quickly due to a translation error.*"

The story there was that the Minister of Information couldn't read English, so he had the articles translated for him and the quality of the translation wasn't always great and in stressful conditions of work. I was told once that one translator had a stapler thrown at his head as he interpreted what *Yemen Times* published – maybe to put things together better using the stapler, the joke goes. I'd – very much – like to sympathize with the translator, but I still get a chuckle every time I remember this story.

That ordeal revealed a lot about the impact of *Yemen Times* on the highest levels of political life, and how the President and senior officials related to *Yemen Times* and me. The President and this Minister of Information went way back. In fact, Saleh came to power in 1978, and the current Minister of Information was first appointed in that capacity in 1980 and had been rotating on all sorts of posts over the last two decades. Both of these men seemed to have a lot in common, including hating my guts, and I was not particularly a big fan of either of them either. The silver lining here was that I got to know Aallow much better in the process, learning about his tactics and strategies. I was looking forwards to seeing what seven rabbits he would pull out of his hat this time.

"*My first point begs the question why are we here? Are we here to seek the truth or to give Dr Abdulaziz a hard time to punish his patriotism and concern for Yemen's welfare?*"

"*Unacceptable, Your Honor,*" Prosecutor Abdullah interrupted just as the crowd jittered.

I could see a wide mixture of emotions in the faces around me. Most were friendly and sympathetic, yet I tended to disregard them and eyeballed those who were just plain angry. They were not used to seeing someone standing up against the system, so publicly, and forcing it to jump through hoops like in this trial. They were the ones most annoyed by Aallow's performance, a performance that reached new levels that day. I just hoped we would make it out of there in one piece. I had made lunch plans with a few colleagues at AlShaibani restaurant. I love that place and the ambiance takes me back to the days of my youth.

"*This trial is not about Dr Abdulaziz, it is about the law and the respect to our institutions,*" said Abdullah.

The judge was quick to slam the table with his hand. Things seemed to be getting out of control. In fact, getting out of hand was an understatement. This was supposed to be a delicate, friendly, smooth-sailing session. All I wanted to do was prove the point that someone needed to be held accountable for the mismanagement and outright embezzlement of this poor country's resources. This shameless theft needed to be checked.

"*I've heard enough. I decided this matter is to go for a full trial. You will hear from the court on the next session date. We are adjourned.*"

Aallow was quick to interject. "*Your Honor, I have an urgent and important request...*"

"*WHAT?*" the judge demanded.

"*I need the court to order personal protection for Dr Abdulaziz due to the threats...*"

The judge was quick to interrupt as he stood up from his seat. "*Request denied.*"

I didn't see this abrupt end coming, in fact I was daydreaming during the trial about my tribulations that got me here. How journalism had become such a high mortality job. In fact, in January, I had made a public appeal to President Saleh following the language against me in State media. The one that alarmed me most was the statement on the cover of an armed forces newspaper managed by the press Secretary of the President saying "... Saqqaf is working his way to suicide...." Should I be worried? Of course I was worried. I didn't want to continue doing this if it would cost me my life.

I saw Aallow shaking hands with Abdullah, a customary move, but I also saw Aallow's face change. Something was not right. Aallow rushed to me asking for the keys to my car. I was not sure why he wanted them, but when I gave him the keys, he gave them to one of his staffers and said, "*Go check the car. Bring it inside and wait for us.*"

Aallow held my hand and escorted me through the crowd; usually he wasn't this overprotective. People were flocking in and out of the courtroom, being prepared for the next session. The rule of thumb was that the second case usually waited by the door when the first finished and so on. Our tired judicial system had little capacity, although the widespread injustices touched more people every day.

Aallow had a guard open an office for us at the end of the corridor. We walked in. It looked like an abandoned office with furniture from different eras of the building's history, which seemed to be used by lawyers and defendants to consult. It spoke to the state of this nation.

"*Abdulaziz... I am worried for you. You heard the judge, he denied the request*," Aallow said

"*Yeah, but they always deny that request, don't they?*"

"*No,*" Aallow said. "*They defer such requests usually. In your case, he said No.*" He added, "*Do you know what that means? Do you know that Abdullah told me: 'Tell your friend to take care of himself.' Do you know what that means, Abdulaziz?*"

Aallow's tone of voice was different this time. He knew something was not right. He was the lawyer for many human rights activists and had grown to predict the future of human rights activists. The future of the fallen.

"*Abdulaziz,*" he said, "*listen to me. You will buy a ticket and fly out of here today for a couple of days. You can come back when the situation cools. What do you think the big guy will do when he receives the report from this session? You think he will let it go?*"

"*But I made lunch plans...*"

"*ABDULAZIZ!*" Aallow yelled, gesturing disapproval. Then a moment of silence followed.

I tried to comfort him telling him everything would be alright. I needed to brush it off and told Aallow that I was having an important working lunch in preparation for the upcoming forum.

"*Don't worry about me, I have organized an important lunch meeting...*"

Aallow interrupted me dismissively saying, "*Go on then, get out of here.*"

This was certainly no ordinary day. I had stepped over many lines before in my career in pursuit of what I thought was right. I stepped on some powerful and influential toes. I got my share of threats, beatings, nights in jail. The two responses by *26 September* and *Al-Mithaq* to the $22.5 billion article were particularly crude and painful. But this was new to me.

As I was walking through the corridors out of the courtroom, it felt like I'd just advanced into a higher level of difficulty in my maneuvering with the regime, and needed more expert-level guidance, especially with Aallow's worrying advice. More importantly, I needed to think about what I would say to my wife Aziza when she asked how things went. Also, how would I recount this trial experience in a forthcoming editorial of *Yemen Times*.

Suddenly, I noticed I was being followed, so I sped up my steps and looked around for familiar faces. I found no one I knew, just strangers with frowny faces carrying around papers in files or plastic sacks. So I decided to stop and confront the person following me.

"*Ya doctor Abdulaziz, ya doctor Abdulaziz,*" a young fellow appeared with my car keys. That's right. He was Aallow's staffer who brought my car into the compound. Only judges, court administrators, and lawyers were allowed to park inside the compound, which is probably why Aallow sent his staffer to bring my car. Maybe another shake-down was waiting for me outside and it was better to drive off straight from the compound.

"*Thanks, son.*"

We shook hands and he walked away quickly, probably in a hurry to attend another trial. Aallow was a busy man and his legal practice was in high demand. He got things done. But a grave thought hit me: *Maybe Aallow thought a car-bomb was rigged to my car and was okay with sacrificing his staffer? Probably not. What am I thinking? This is 1999, not 1982.*

When I reached my car, I was approached by the court's janitor-turned-guard. He looked at least seventy years old from the wrinkles on his face; he probably started working here before this building was first constructed, seeing all sorts of people and cases walk through these doors.

"*This is your car or Aallow's car? Every day he has a new car,*" he said.

"*Ya Hala ya Hajj,*" I replied to him in a friendly manner. "*How are you? Actually, this is my car.*"

"We thank God for the blessing of good health. But I have three boys who are a big pain; they can't find work and they stay at home all day. You look like you can hire one of them," the guard said. "*I'm already tired, so tired,*" he added.

Me too, I thought.

"*Here, Hajj, this is for you, from Aallow.*" I handed him three thousand Riyals, just under twenty dollars.

As I got in my car, he was praying for my safety and to win the case I was involved in. Obviously, this old man knew how to read faces, and knew what kind of prayer was needed in which case. To my surprise, I found the boxes of paper that Aallow's staffers presented in the courtroom. I was curious to see what was inside, and I found documentation for several other old cases and what looked like filler paper. I smiled, realizing that it was all a stunt, and this was probably why he didn't leave it around as he knew it would be found and searched.

It took me twenty minutes of driving in and around traffic with my own thoughts before I realized that I hadn't turned on the radio in the car. I always turned on the radio when I drove, especially with my plans to launch my own radio station in the near future.

Chapter 20: The Final Lunch

Snapping out of that, thanks to my grumbling stomach, I found my parking spot across the street from AlShaibani restaurant. This meeting had been in the works for quite some time and was a big deal given the upcoming Emerging Democracies Forum.

I was a late arrival to the lunch gathering. As I walked in, I was welcomed by Nabil, the all-in-one manager, doorman, and troubleshooter for the restaurant. Nabil was a middle-aged, stubby-looking guy, wearing traditional dress while sitting cross-legged on top of a table at the entrance with a hawk-like view over the dining hall on one side, and the door and the street on the other. Next to him was his trusted beige rotary phone, a blue Bic pen hung on a string from the wall, and his die-hard handrest-turned-desk with a file jammed between it and the wall.

Nabil said: "*Hayaa Allah bel-doctor,*" a traditionally flattering way of welcoming someone, literally meaning that blessings accompany you. "*Your people are here and are waiting upstairs,*" telling me that some VIP-looking people asked for Abdulaziz's table, and were escorted to the much-quieter section on the second floor of the restaurant.

Although I was the one who organized this working lunch, I was the last to arrive. Around the table were four men, all in suits. On the right was a senior advisor on democracy who covered Yemen, among other countries. He had been shuffling in and out, as they were our partners in co-organizing the Emerging Democracies Forum, but he was always up-to-date and always on point. Next to him was their representative in Yemen, a trusted American who had an exceptionally good organizational sense. The third person was a colleague and a bright mind, serving as the Minister of Labor for Yemen but he had shown genuine interest in making a meaningful contribution to solving Yemen's problems. He was quite keen on this meeting and appreciative of my efforts to organize it. He is also key to influencing, and being influenced, by this working lunch. The fourth was Dr Abu Baker, a longtime friend and colleague from my first days at Sana'a University. He was well connected with different parts of the regime, politically savvy, and an excellent wingman in such settings.

"*First things first, did you guys order?*" I asked. Apparently they were waiting for me, given I picked the venue and organized the meeting. After the order was placed, we went into our discussion.

"*Yemen may be a poor country in a rich neighborhood, but we have made fantastic headway in building a modern democracy compared to our neighbors,*" I started by saying. My point was to go out of our way to ensure good regional representation in the upcoming event. Then I wondered; *Do I tell them about the Saudi operative who attended my trial this morning? Maybe not.*

It was a working lunch and the discussion was focused. And we were going over the key outcome messages expected and what they would mean for Yemen and the region. We knew many regional elements would be happy to see Yemen's experience flop, which is why we needed all the handholding and high-level political messaging we could get.

We concluded our lunch with a long to-do list, largely in terms of the media package to cover the event and the congratulatory notes we wanted President Saleh to receive on the success of the event following its conclusion. We needed to maintain momentum and keep up the pressure, especially given current backsliding. I told them of recent happenings and tightening political space to drive this point home and we agreed on some concrete next steps and our next meeting. The meeting adjourned, we went our separate ways.

Then it happened.

I was struck by a speeding vehicle as I was standing on the middle island waiting to cross the road to my parked car. I flew into the air and landed on my side several yards away. At first, I heard the thud noise from my body hitting the car, then passed out momentarily, probably due to the pain of my landing. I was trying to get up, feeling the hot tarmac on my palm and face. Then I was moved. I was not sure if good Samaritans were trying to revive me and take me to the hospital, or if it was a kidnapping gone wrong. I heard chaotic mumbling, I tasted blood, I felt my pain getting numb. This was my time to go.

I never got to say goodbye to my family and loved ones, my team in *Yemen Times*, my students, and partners in democracy, and all those I cared about. But I hope this will help - for my peace and yours. Goodbye.

Afterward

The body arrived at Al-Thawra Hospital around an hour after the accident, where he was pronounced dead on arrival. The family of Dr Abdulaziz Al-Saqqaf was notified about the accident two hours later.

Dr Abdulaziz's car was taken to an undisclosed location and searched. The boxes that Aallow's assistant left in the car were visibly roughed up, and the family was asked to collect the car six hours later from a traffic stop near *Yemen Times*'s office.

The case against *Yemen Times* and Dr Al-Saqqaf regarding the $22.5 billion story was dropped, citing the demise of the opponent. President Saleh won the 1999 Presidential elections with 96.2% of the vote.

The driver of the car was apprehended by passers-by, and an investigation committee was formed, headed by the Minister of Interior. Some twenty-one irregularities with the investigation resulted in a blotched process and a mistrial. Dr Abdulaziz's family decided to abandon the case.

Dr Abdulaziz was buried at the Martyrs' cemetery in Sana'a. Vice President Hadi and a large number of senior officials and activists attended the funeral service, along with family, friends, and *Yemen Times* staff.

The Emergent Democracies Forum took place later in June, and included a moment of silence for Dr Abdulaziz. His work and contributions were widely recognized, and he was awarded the Lifetime Achievement award from the Dubai-based Middle East Publishers Conference.

Walid took the helm of *Yemen Times* and continued in his father's footsteps. His era included important growth in *Yemen Times*, including publishing twice a week and acquiring its own printing press. Nadia took over several years later.

Aziza passed away the year after Dr Abdulaziz.

Interview with Aziza
June 14, 1999

The whole country was shocked and saddened by the loss of Dr Abdulaziz Al-Saqqaf, the publisher of Yemen Times. Not only Yemenis, but also Arabs and foreigners were depressed by this horrible development. But among all of these people there was one person who was saddened the most – his life companion, Mrs Aziza Al-Saqqaf. Aziza is the mother of two boys and two girls; namely, Haifa, Walid, Nadia, and Raydan. She is forty-five years old and was born in the Al-Hadharem village in rural Taiz. Aziza is the person who joined Dr Abdulaziz in building his, life brick by brick. She is the person who witnessed his good and bad times, his prosperous and needy times, and, most important of all, his successes and failures. Aziza looks like any common Yemeni middle-aged lady who comes from a good family. Yet all you need is to talk to her once to realize what a remarkable person she is. It's enough for her that she is the late Dr Al-Saqqaf's wife. Yemen Times talked to Mrs Aziza and filed the following interview.

Q: First of all, we offer our condolence for the death of your husband, Dr Abdulaziz Al-Saqqaf. Could you give us a brief of how this happened?
A: On Wednesday evening, the 2nd of July 1999, I was waiting for my husband to come back from a lunch meeting with a few of his

friends. He promised to come back from lunch before going back to work in the afternoon. When I noticed that he is late, I began to feel disturbed and worried that something might have happened to him. I told my elder son Walid to call the office and ask whether he is there or not. He called and couldn't find him. So I waited for one more hour before I demanded that Walid send a person from the *Yemen Times* office to go and ask the restaurant about him. At 3:50, Walid went to the office as usual. Then I received a telephone call from one of my husband's friends saying that he was in the hospital because of an accident. I then fell unconscious. After some time, I woke up to find my son Walid saying, "Dad is alive and will stay alive in our hearts. Don't worry, Mom, I am here beside you, and I always stay here." I then realized that everything was all over, I had lost my husband. Later I found out that he was hit by a speeding car while crossing the street. The accident was fatal, and he died. May God have mercy upon his soul.

Q: *What do you think of the accident?*
A: As I understood from the Traffic Police report, the accident seems unintentional, but the investigations are still underway. I just want the driver to be punished severely for he killed my beloved husband, and nothing in the whole world can be substituted for him. All we can do now is pray for him, that God will let his soul rest in heaven.

Q: *We pray for him too. Let us now go back in time. When and how did you marry Dr Al-Saqqaf?*
A: We lived in the same village. I was quite young then, around nineteen years old. After he finished high school in Taiz, he proposed for me, and my father and I accepted him, and we got married and moved to Sana'a. It was merely a coincidence that our names are similar, but it was our destiny to get married and live a happy life together.

Q: *What about your life after marriage, how was it affected?*

A: After staying a while in Sana'a with my husband, my husband was granted a scholarship from the Washington-based Fulbright Associations. We then traveled to the USA and my husband enrolled in a PhD program there, and I obtained a diploma there in teaching English as a second language.

Q: Are you a housewife?
A: No, I do have a job. After returning to Yemen the second time in 1985, I started teaching English at Khowla School. I am still a teacher there today, and I will try to continue teaching even after my husband's death.

Q: You seem to have visited many countries with your husband. Did that effect your attitude generally?
A: Very much. Anyone who travels out of Yemen and sees the world around him/her, he/she realizes the true dimensions of his/her country's ranking in the world. Unfortunately, whenever I am away, I feel sorry for my country.

Q: So, what have you done for your country so far?
A: I haven't done much. But I believe I raised my children to become very beneficial to their country, just like their father. I assure you that time will tell how well they have been raised. I also do my job as a teacher honestly. I am a member of many charities. I helped my husband a lot in improving our village. One of my most influential contributions to my rural area in Al-Hadharem was the establishing and running of the Al-Hadharem Women Vocational Training Center.

Q: Can you tell us more about this center?
A: The center was established in 1994. It had three sections: stitching, literacy, and household. Registration and enrollment in the center was absolutely free of charge. The lessons provided were in two shifts, five days a week. We had many students coming from all over the region. I was the principal and tried hard to make the center as organized and influential as possible. The center distributed authorized certificates. I am happy to tell you that many of our students found jobs because of the training they obtained at our center. Some of them even have designed and produced their own goods, which were sold fairly cheaply. We also used to offer the students of the center monthly supplies of flour, sugar, milk, oil, cheese, peas, and other goods, all for free. It was a great hassle trying to manage all that as well as discipline but with God's support and hard work it was a clear success.

Q: Did you face any difficulties being Dr Al-Saqqaf's wife?
A: Yes and no. He was a very busy man. He was so busy that his children would sometimes not see him in the house the whole day. I remember that my youngest child, Ray, once asked me if his father was out of Sana'a because he hadn't seen him for three consecutive days. I had to do everything myself. Taking care of the children, going to work, managing the house, and receiving my husband's guests were all part of my duty. Nevertheless, all of that gave me pleasure. I felt that the hectic life I led gave my world a colorful meaning. I knew my time was spent on something useful instead of nothing. Many Yemeni wives use their leisure in spending long hours in useless chatting with other women. But I am a person who isn't used to doing that because our life style forced us to find more useful things to do. Having my husband, the late Dr Al-Saqqaf, as our idol, we built an ideal kind of life, which we should always thank him for.

Q: Do you face any difficulty now that your husband has passed away?
A: Of course! Our loss is not small. We are now trying to cope with our life without my husband. But it is certainly not easy. As Dr Al-Saqqaf's family, we are doing all we can to try and be strong and stick together all the time. We will do it, not only for our own sake, but for the sake of making my beloved husband feel proud that he raised us so well that we could depend on ourselves and carry on life without weakening or giving up. He taught us how to be strong and survive in any circumstance. We cherish his memories and the least we can do now is to keep his spirit among us and to carry on life without him, but with all the lessons he taught us.

Q: What does Yemen Times mean to you?
A: In the beginning, I was annoyed at the idea of establishing a newspaper in English. I knew that it would be a difficult task to accomplish, and I thought of the possibility of the state shutting it down for his courageous and frank articles that might not please the leaders. But later on I began to get used to it. I remember I used to cry about his leaving us early in the morning and coming at night! Most of the time he wouldn't even have his meals at home as if home had turned to a hotel or something. Whenever he released a dangerous article in the front page of the paper, we used to feel worried that trouble might result from it. My husband liked *Yemen Times* so much that sometimes I got jealous of it. I even had a thought of it as his second wife! After years and years of hard work, my husband started to be heard, and I would feel the pride in his eyes when he discovered that his messages reached millions of readers in the world. I began to like everything he did and started to appreciate his efforts. In fact, I felt equally responsible for continuing *Yemen Times* and strengthening it. He used to say it was his third daughter, and I used to get irritated. Now I agree, and we will never give it up.

Q: Are there any regrets?
A: I do regret the whole situation of my country. I love Yemen and it hurts to see what it is like today. I keep wishing everything would be right and that Yemen would catch up with the first world countries and become "Alyamen Alsaidah" – happy Yemen. I do regret the situation of the unimplemented laws in the country. If traffic laws were implemented, would my husband still be beside me? I do not want other people to suffer because of the corruption in the country and the ineffectiveness in implementing the laws in this country. I lost my husband and don't want other women to lose theirs. The government and leadership must stand up to what is happening and try to implement the rules, for the sake of our children's future.

Q: How do you think rules in Yemen could be respected and implemented?
A: If everybody does his/her job promptly and honestly, I think that should be enough. Yemen doesn't lack resources. I'm also sorry that deforestation has become more apparent day after day. I do my share as I have planted trees around my house and hope everybody does that too. If only Yemenis would work instead of chewing qat, we could do something good for the country. I met many Yemenis abroad who were successful people and respected in their fields. They all think that qat is the reason behind Yemenis' troubles. I wish all those Yemeni talents were to be utilized by the government in their own country instead of somewhere else.

Q: Any closing statement?
A: The whole of Yemen was saddened by the loss of Dr Al-Saqqaf. I want you to all to try and fight for his goals, fight for his principles, and try to be courageous and never fear death. For the only thing one can get out of this world is one's work. As the late stated "the basic source of wealth should be one's work." Take care of yourselves by taking care of your country. You never know what tomorrow will bring. Stay clean mentally as well as physically. Stop

wasting your time and get going. Do something fruitful, you will eventually gain the fruit. I believe that there still are many Yemenis who stand for the truth without fearing anyone anytime. As long as these people exist, I know that Dr Abdulaziz is still alive and will never die.

If you enjoyed reading this book, please leave a review at *Amazon.com*. It will help others find this book and learn about Dr Abdulaziz's story. Thank you.

www.ingramcontent.com/pod-product-compliance
Lightning Source LLC
LaVergne TN
LVHW011418080426
835512LV00005B/130